PRIMITIVE AND FOLK
JEWELRY

PRIMITIVE AND FOLK
JEWELRY

EDITED BY MARTIN GERLACH

INTRODUCTION AND CAPTIONS BY
MICHAEL HABERLANDT
Late Curator at the
Naturhistorisches Museum, Vienna

DOVER PUBLICATIONS, INC.
NEW YORK

Published in Canada by General Publishing Company, Ltd., 30 Lesmill Road, Don Mills, Toronto, Ontario.
Published in the United Kingdom by Constable and Company, Ltd., 10 Orange Street, London WC 2.

This Dover edition, first published in 1971, is an unabridged translation of the work *Völkerschmuck, mit besonderer Berücksichtigung des metallischen Schmuckes,* originally published by the Verlag von Gerlach & Wiedling, Vienna and Leipzig, n.d. (Introduction dated 1906), as volume number VII in the series *Die Quelle.* This new translation was prepared specially for the present edition.

International Standard Book Number: 0-486-22747-2
Library of Congress Catalog Card Number: 70-125624

Manufactured in the United States of America
Dover Publications, Inc.
180 Varick Street
New York, N. Y. 10014

Introduction

The present work, which includes material from the jewelry of all mankind, is offered to the public by Martin Gerlach primarily as a collection of models for the creative art of the goldsmith, as a treasury of motifs and source of inspiration for ever new inventiveness in the precious field of personal adornment. In the series of similar publications ("Die Quelle") which the Vienna art publishers Gerlach & Wiedling have already made available for the enrichment and refinement of the artistic and applied art production of the present day (now that, after a long standstill, a new artistic will is again stirring), a contribution concerning jewelry could least of all be omitted; for it is precisely jewelry which, by its very nature and costliness inclining more than any other item of human utility toward stagnation of form and being least subject to the restlessness of fashion, needs from time to time, and today more than ever, an artistic freshening and an infusion of new inventiveness and proven attractiveness.

Moreover, through the great number of jewelry forms from all nations and periods reproduced in it, the present work gains a certain value for the history and ethnography of the jewelry of mankind, although this was not expressly intended and no special ethnographic claims are made. It is clear from the very lack of any such arrangement in this book (this can be sufficiently explained and excused by the laborious method of assembling the work, whose pages had to be brought together gradually over many years from numerous museums and private collections all over Europe) that the ethnographic significance of the volume can be regarded only as a welcome secondary acquisition. Its true purpose, to which all else had to be subordinated, is the enrichment of modern production, the broadening of taste in ornament in the goldsmith's art of today and especially in the public, which must be gradually educated to view the best qualities of jewelry not merely in the bare abstract costliness of the material—as in the case of diamonds—but above all in the nobility and richness of the form, in the liveliness of the invention, in the multiplicity and the individuality of the styles of decoration. It cannot be overlooked that precisely in this field a lamentable artistic impoverishment has made itself felt. All previous eras have far surpassed the present in their fine sensibility to artistic values in jewelry, as both body ornament and clothing ornament. The jewelry legacy of perished nations, down to the peasant jewelry of the various European countries; the jewelry of the Orient, kaleidoscopic in form and color; even the primitive decorative arts of the less advanced non-white peoples—not to mention the artistic nobility of the jewelry of classical antiquity—all possess in an outstanding degree what we lack today more and more and what we must achieve again: fullness and originality of invention, definite ideals in jewelry leading to the development of fixed ensemble patterns, taste and fine feeling for the spiritual and ethical elements that are innate in jewelry alongside its esthetic charm. In this regard, too, the dissolution of the old social order—of classes, great families and guilds —and the democratization of taste have chiefly evoked an irremediable leveling and shallowness in which primarily the material—monetary—value of jewelry has become the key point in production and demand.

The jewelry of mankind has from the earliest times developed in a twofold direction: as *body ornament* and as *clothing ornament*. The unclothed peoples or those who possess the so-called subtropical costume, which leaves great parts of the body uncovered, have developed body ornament in a multitude of forms, leaving no part of the body that could possibly bear jewelry without its artificial adornment; the clothed peoples, on the other hand, have brought to its full development clothing ornament, which is worn over and largely in the service of clothing, to keep individual pieces, wraps, etc., in place. Both types of jewelry have become utilized everywhere in typical, more or less fixed patterns of *"jewel costumes"* or *sets of jewelry*. It is a characteristic of all primitive and older articles of jewelry that they have no individual self-sufficient significance, that they are not worn arbitrarily according to individual taste and caprice, in any number and arrangement, as jewelry is used today, but that the individual types of jewelry count only as components of an established, developed and complicated ensemble, just as costumes everywhere originally formed a consistent whole which was dissolved only gradually with the passage of time. In all primitive and all older periods of jewelry the individual jewelry form, such as the earring, necklace or ring, is not to be considered as complete in itself; instead —and especially on festive occasions of private and social life, when body ornament makes its most frequent and its fullest appearance—one always finds more or less determined jewelry ensembles that form an artistic whole. Unfortunately, this important fact has hitherto been almost completely overlooked in the research and depiction of the jewelry of the world's peoples. Museums house in their collections for the most part only individual pieces of jewelry torn from their context, without regard for their organic relationship to larger or complex jewelry ensembles. Only in the rarest instances up to now has jewelry been collected and displayed in museums with this point of view; only the ethnological museums offered, in part, a praiseworthy exception in this regard. Considering this state of affairs, we must be excused if in the present work too this point of view could hardly be adhered to, desirable as that would have been in the interest of creative production, which will have to occupy itself not only with the invention of new individual jewelry forms, but also with the composition of new modern jewelry ensembles and jewelry ideals.

A swift glance at the great number of plates in the present work shows that the entire development of the jewelry of mankind is unfurled here, from the pre-metallic jewelry of primitive peoples through prehistoric bronze jewelry and the jewelry of the ancients, down to its last offshoots in the present-day peasant jewelry of the European nations. But the prevailing point of view of the editor, Martin Gerlach, in his choice of these specimens from all these eras and regions was, as I have emphasized, not a scholarly one—to show historical development—but a practical one; in each case he sought those forms and examples which by their appropriate application of form to material, their excellence in design and color combination, their moderation and nobility of invention, seemed most apt to enrich the imagination of modern workers in this field and broaden their taste. *Not in the sense of direct patterns, however, to be simply copied slavishly,* but as models and samples of feeling for style and of that faithful workmanship which does its best to transform the ornamental idea it has conceived into splendid and shining reality.

For perfect transparency and simplicity here are, first of all, the models and samples from the pre-metallic cultures: several plates are filled with interesting and charming articles of jewelry from the South Seas and the Negro cultures. Here jewelry is still very closely connected with the economic circumstances of the peoples, and the division of jewelry between the sexes unmistakably reflects the division of labor between them. Their adornment is thoroughly a *jewelry of nature,* produced by the men from the yield of their hunting—from feathers, teeth, claws, bone, tortoise-shell, pelts—and quite laboriously assembled by the women chiefly from plant material, bright berries, seeds, grass stalks, but also from sea shells and snail shells, that is, precisely from the realm of their other labor and production.

Gradually metal supplants natural ornament—as it supplants natural objects in the field of weapons and tools, and probably earlier than in those fields for the most part—and replaces it with *metal jewelry,* that true ornament of the civilized world. One group of plates presents a large number of prehistoric jewelry forms from the early periods of this development; the material is bronze. It has already been repeatedly observed that the world of prehistoric design—especially in its Bronze Age developments—shows a strange affinity in design to the most modern directions in taste and their most modern products. Truly, modern designers will gain valuable lessons from a language of forms such as that exemplified by the Hallstatt culture, for instance, so just in its handling of the material, so severe in style.

This brief presentation of prehistoric jewelry forms marks just the beginning of a study (probably to become more and more intensive) of this extremely individual and rich prehistoric world of European design, which hitherto has unjustly remained a sort of *terra incognita* to artistic production.

The jewelry of the ancient world, which in the East, in Greece, Italy, and finally again in Byzantium enjoyed a development so rich, manifold and funda-mental to the history of jewelry, is shown in the present work in a number of outstanding and singular examples. Special attention has been given to less well-known material from these schools of design.

The solid and skillful goldsmith's art of *Egypt* with its never-failing sensitivity to style and its special technical peculiarities, such as the inlay technique, frequently based on religious forms, has received appropriate consideration.

The refined jewelry of the Greeks, which in its artistic treatment was in the highest accord with the principle of suitability of form to material, is here represented by some of the famous gold hoards from the Crimea. Also illustrated are a great number of splendid finds—of exemplary value—from the rich storehouse of *Etruscan* jewelry, which sprang from a highly developed, technically complex jeweler's art, which had to provide for the living and the dead equally. And finally, *Roman jewelry,* which like Roman culture in general combined the legacy of the Eastern, Greek and Etruscan worlds, furnished a significant portion of the illustrations.

For the jewelry of the era of barbaric invasions (*Völkerwanderung*) and the early Middle Ages, in so far as it has been considered in the present work, the reader is referred primarily to the magnificent gold hoards housed in the Hungarian National Museum in Budapest, and to Byzantine forms, which survive to a great extent in the folk art of the Balkan countries.

Outside the cultural frame of reference of the Old World lie the well-known prehistoric gold jewelry hoards coming from the Central and South American Indians—which in their altogether prehistoric techniques display primitive forms of completely unspoiled charm—as well as a group of jewelry items from the older Negro cultures, such as the well-known Benin finds and some products of the Ashanti, who have already undergone southern European influence.

By far the greatest number of objects included here have been drawn from the jewelry of the last two centuries in *Asia* and *Europe.*

In Asia we can distinguish a series of more or less clear regions or provinces of jewelry, which coincide essentially with the most important spheres of Asiatic culture. These are on Asiatic soil: the East Asian jewelry province, to which belong the completely individual jewelry ensembles of China, Korea and Japan; the Indian jewelry zone with its offshoot in the Malay Archipelago, perhaps the most perfect and flourishing development that human creativity in jewelry has attained anywhere on earth; the Upper Asian jewelry zone, to which belongs the jewelry of the Himalayan countries, Mongolia and parts of Siberia; and finally the Near Eastern, which displays Persian, Syrian-Arabic and Turkish schools of design alongside one another. Each of these jewelry provinces are characteristically distinct in materials, design and ornament. They are all very fully represented here.

The transition to the jewelry of the *European peoples* in modern times is to be found in the rich stores of folk jewelry that the peoples of the Balkan peninsula (especially the women) display generously to the present day on their holiday costumes. Wherever the national jewelry of the European peoples has been presented in this work an especially prominent place has been accorded to peasant jewelry in the conviction that here, too, there still remains an untapped wealth of delightful ornament and solid design which can be made fruitful for the present generation. The European jewelry here presented comes mainly from the eighteenth and the first half of the nineteenth centuries. Only exceptionally do the objects go back to earlier eras. As for the choice of individual items, we remind the reader once more that this book attempts to provide a swift survey, not an exhaustive review, of European production.

In the production of the present work the editor Martin Gerlach enjoyed the kind cooperation of numerous museums and private collectors, who not only freely permitted him to photograph various greater and smaller groups of jewelry items in their possession, but also very kindly supplied the data for the description of the plates, which in accordance with the practical purpose of the volume had to be kept as brief as possible. The editor is only fulfilling a pleasant and deeply felt duty in publicly stating his warmest and sincerest thanks to the following authorities, museum directors and collectors:

The K. K. Oberstkämmereramt in Vienna; the Directors of the K. K. Naturhistorisches Museum in Vienna; the Directors of the K. K. Kunsthistorisches Museum in Vienna; the Directors of the K. K. Österreichisches Museum für Kunst und Industrie in Vienna; of the Museum für Österreichische Volkskunde in Vienna; of the Kunstgewerbeschule in Vienna; of the Moravian Commerce Museum in Brünn (Brno); of the Czechoslovakian Ethnographical Museum and Náprstek Museum in Prague; of the North Bohemian Commerce Museum in Reichenberg (Liberec); of the Hungarian National Museum and Regional Applied Art Museum in Budapest; of the Königliches Kunstgewerbe-Museum and the Museum für Völkerkunde in Berlin; of the Schlesisches Museum für Kunstgewerbe und Altertümer in Breslau; of the Kunstgewerbe-Museum and the Museum für Völkerkunde in Dresden; of the Grossherzoglich Badische Sammlung für Altertümer und Völkerkunde in Karlsruhe; of the Königliche Zeichen-Akademie in Hanau; of the Museum für Länder- und Völkerkunde in Stuttgart; of the Neue Pinakothek in Munich; of the Kunstgewerbe-Museum and the Germanisches Museum in Nuremberg; of the Museum für Kunst und Gewerbe in Hamburg; of the Gewerbe-Museum in Bremen; of the Neues Städtisches Museum in Braunschweig; of the Museum für Völkerkunde in Leipzig; of the Landes-Museum in Zurich; of the Louvre in Paris; of the British Museum in London; of the National Museum of Antiquities of Scotland, Edinburgh; his Excellency Count Karl Lanckoroński, Vienna; H. Tarnay, Vienna; the late Amalie Schönchen, actress of the Imperial Theater, Vienna; Privy Councillor M. Rosenberg; Karlsruhe; Theodor Heiden, court jeweler, Munich; A. Merklein, goldsmith, Nuremberg; C. Esslinger, postal director, Leer; Tillmann-Schmitt, Breslau; T. Schmitz, engraver, Breslau; Frau von Minkwitz, Breslau; E. Voetz, Haarlem; Dr. Focke, Bremen.

If the present work contains, as we hope it does, any lasting value for the improvement and enrichment of the goldsmith's art and in general for artistic and scholarly interest in the jewelry of mankind and its development, thanks are primarily due to the above-named museums and collectors, whose finest privilege it remains to reawaken new life from dead things.

Vienna, September 1906   DR. M. HABERLANDT
                                      Curator of the Ethnographic Collection
                                      of the K. K. Naturhistorisches Hofmuseum.

LIST OF ILLUSTRATIONS

(arranged by place of origin of the articles)

Pre-metallic Jewelry

Metal Jewelry

PREHISTORIC TIMES

ANTIQUITY

MODERN TIMES: ASIA

MODERN TIMES: AFRICA

MODERN TIMES: AMERICA

MODERN TIMES: EUROPE

PRIMITIVE AND FOLK
JEWELRY

Plate 1

1. Bronze necklace. Bulgaria (Sofia).

2. Hair ornament of bronze plate. Bulgaria (Jambol).

3. Bronze curtain clasp. Kragujevac (Topolja).

4, 5. Breast ornament, whitish alloy. 18th century. Bulgaria (Sofia).

6. "Tepelik" (knob for headgear), with Turkish silver coins. Bulgaria (Zagora).

7. Belt buckle of gilded metal, gold filigree. Bulgaria (Kotel).

8. Bronze arm bracelet. Bulgaria (Eskisagra).

9. Earring of whitish metal. Bulgaria (Trnova).

10. Arm band of silver gilt. Bulgaria (Kirkilisse).

11. Earring, silver hook with old Serbian copper coins. Bulgaria.

12. Belt ornament of silver alloy, filigree, brass chain; bridal ornament. Serbia.

13. Brass clasps. Bulgaria.

14. Cap ornament, silver with slight gilding. Bulgaria (Sofia).

15. Necklace. Bulgaria (Zagora).

16. Belt buckle of whitish alloy. Bulgaria.

17. Brass belt buckle. Bulgaria.

18. Belt clasp of whitish alloy. Bulgaria.

19. Necklace, silver chain with old Serbian copper coins in the shape of bowls worn by Gypsy girls. Serbia.

(Naturhistorisches Museum, Vienna, Ethnographic Collection.)

Plate 2

1, 3. Earring, silver gilt set with red stones. 18th to 19th century. Greece.

2. Large breast ornament, partly gilded and set with brightly colored stones. 18th to 19th century. Greece.

4, 5. Halves of a breast pendant, silver gilt set with red and green stones. 19th century. Turkey.

6, 8. Earring, gold, enamel and pearls. 18th to 19th century. Greek islands.

7. Necklace of silver filigree, modern. Egypt.
(Kunstgewerbe-Museum, Berlin.)

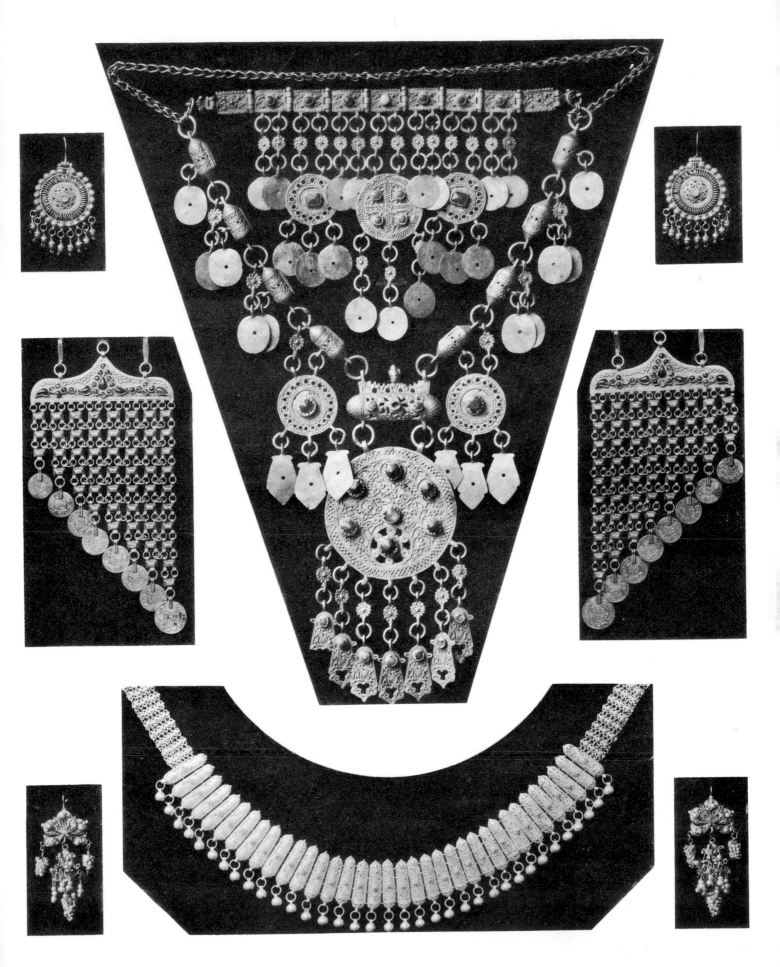

Plate 3

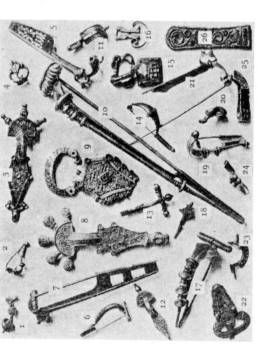

Roman finds:

1. Bowed brooch, set with latticed silver ornaments.
2, 7. Silver fibulas.
3. Bowed brooch, silver, partially gilded.
4. Small buckle, silver.
5. Bowed brooch, gold.
6. Fibula, silver. Csóra, Transylvania.
8. Bronze clothing brooch.
9. Silver clasp.
10. Silver fibula of unusual size.
11, 12. Silver brooches.
13, 14, 24. Bowed brooches, silver.
15. Bronze buckle, gilded, with glass inlays.
16. Fragment of a clasp, silver.
17. Jointed brooch of silver.
18. Iron bowed brooch, covered with gilded silver plate.
19. Bowed brooch, silver. Gross-Pöchlarn, Lower Austria.
20. Silver fibula.
21. Silver fibula. Hochroterd, Lower Austria.
22. Bronze buckle.
23. Silver bowed clasp. Deutsch-Altenburg.
25. Fragment of a clasp, silver.
26. Bronze covering of a belt.
(Kunsthistorisches Museum, Vienna.)

Plate 4

Roman finds:
1. Gold chain with miniature tools. Szilágyisomlyó, Transylvania.
2. Final link of a necklace, gold.
3. Earring. Euxinograd near Varna.
4. Bowed brooch with cross piece, gold.
5, 16. Gold earrings. Trento.
6. Gold earring.
7. Earring with head of Apis, gold.
8, 9. Arm band, gold.
10. Bowed brooch, gold. Ostropasaka, Hungary.
11. Gold ring. Altsohl, Hungary.
12. Bowed brooch, gold. Carniola.
13. Triangular clasp with inset stones and three attached chains, gold. Hungary.
14. Bowed brooch, gold.
15. Earring with woman's head, gold.
(Kunsthistorisches Museum, Vienna.)

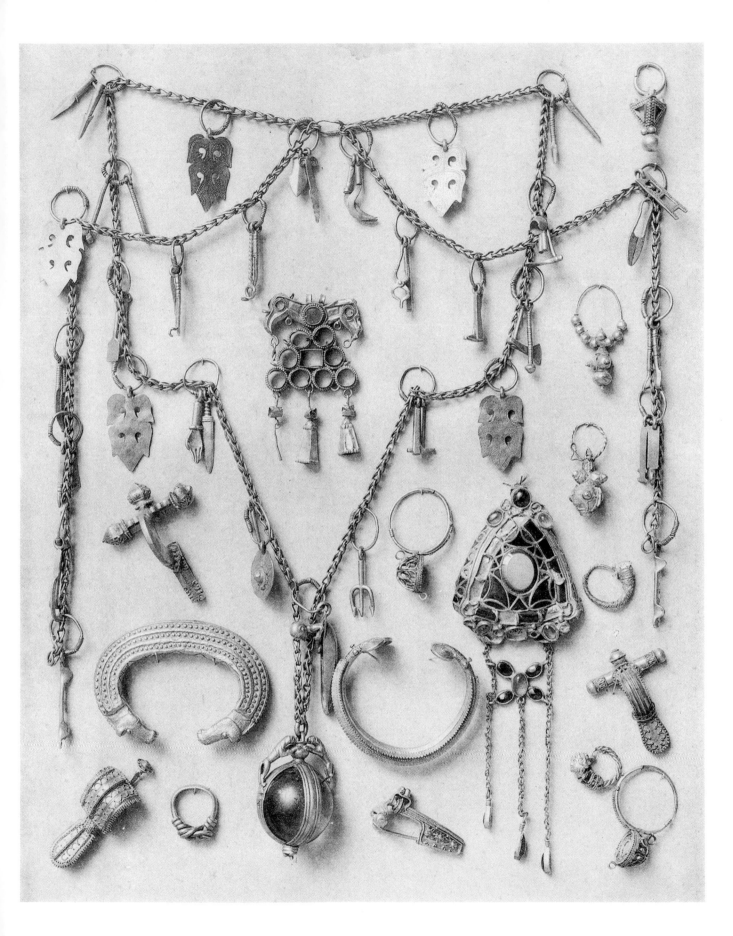

Plate 5

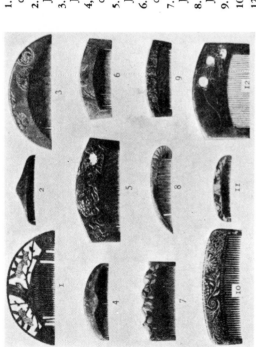

1. Comb, bone, pierced, with reddish gray lacquer. 18th to 19th century. Japan.
2. Comb, tortoise-shell, green and gold. 18th to 19th century. Japan.
3. Comb, wood and painted gold lacquer. 18th to 19th century. Japan.
4, 11. Comb, tortoise-shell with gold lacquer. 18th to 19th century. Japan.
5. Comb, carved wood with mother of pearl. 18th to 19th century. Japan.
6. Comb, wood and gold lacquer with gold plates. 18th to 19th century. Japan.
7. Comb, wood, gold lacquer with coral. 18th to 19th century. Japan.
8. Comb, tortoise-shell, red and gold lacquer. 18th to 19th century. Japan.
9. Comb, wood and red lacquer. 18th to 19th century. Japan.
10. Comb, ivory. 18th to 19th century. Japan.
12. Comb, gold lacquer with colored mother of pearl. 18th to 19th century. Japan.
(Regional Applied Art Museum, Budapest.)

Plate 6

1, 2. Earrings, gilded and set with red stones. 18th to 19th century. Greece.

3. Large breast ornament, partially gilded and set with brightly colored stones. 18th to 19th century. Greece.
(Náprstek Museum, Prague.)

4. Head ornament, silvered metal, with blue and green enamel, set with coral. Syria.

5. Breast ornament, silvered metal, with blue and green enamel, set with coral. Syria.

6. Clasp, silvered metal. Transylvania.

7. Clasps, silvered metal. Syria.

8. Buttons, components of a peasant jewelry ensemble. Norway.
(Moravian Applied Art Museum, Brno.)

Plate 7

1. Breast ornament. Solomon Islands.
2. Neck adornment. Vitu Islands.
3. Nose ornament. New Guinea.
4. Ear jewelry. Solomon Islands.
5. Forehead jewelry. New Guinea, Massilia (Karan).
6. Arm band. New Guinea, [former] Friedrich Wilhelmshafen.
7. Waist band. New Guinea, [former] Krauelbucht.
8. Nose ornament. New Guinea, [former] Berliner-Hafen.
9. Forehead jewelry. New Guinea.
10. Girdle ornament. New Guinea, [former] Friedrich Wilhelms-hafen.
11. Forehead disk. Solomon Islands.
12. Breast ornament. Normanby.
13. Necklace. New Britain.
14. Amulet or ear adornment. New Guinea.
15. Carved ornament. Solomon Islands.
16. Ornament. New Britain.
17. Breast ornament for battle. New Britain.
17A. Waist band. New Guinea.
18. Ear stoppers. Marquesas Islands.
19. Arm band. Sandwich Islands. (Hawaii).
(Naturhistorisches Museum, Vienna, Ethnographic Collection.)

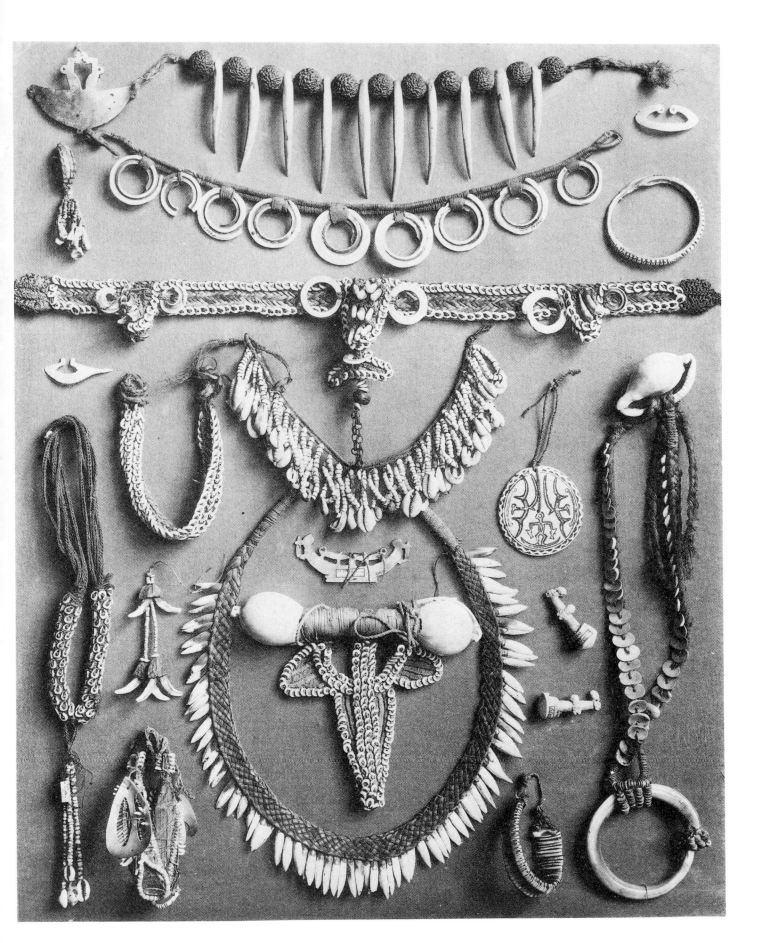

Plate 8

1. Wooden Athos cross in gilded setting. France.
(Collection of Privy Councillor M. Rosenberg, Karlsruhe.)

2, 4, 6, 8. Kap-kap, i. e., bride's breast ornament of Tridacna clam shell with tortoise-shell covering. East coast of New Mecklenburg, Bismarck Archipelago.
(Museum für Länder- und Völkerkunde, Stuttgart.)

3. Ornament from the Arras find, Merovingian. France.
(Collection of Privy Councillor M. Rosenberg, Karlsruhe.)

5. Necklace with silver cylinders and amulet case. Godjamite work. With eight silver bells on silver chains. Debra Markos. Abyssinia, Africa.

7. Brass weight for gold dust. Ashanti, West Africa.
(Museum für Länder- und Völkerkunde, Stuttgart.)

9. Gold enameled plate. India.

10. Gold appliqué for cloth, with pearls. 16th century. Venice.

11. Gold fastener, filigree. Ashanti, West Africa.

12. Wooden Athos cross in a gilded and enameled setting. 15th to 16th century.
(Collection of Privy Councillor M. Rosenberg, Karlsruhe.)

Plate 9

1–20. Tag ends of bodice chains, silver filigree. 19th century. Bavaria, Salzburg and Upper Austria.
(Kunstgewerbe-Museum, Berlin.)

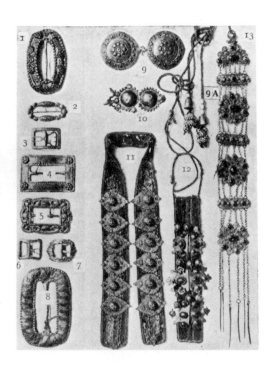

Plate 10

1–8. Belt and shoe buckles, brass and paktong ("German silver"). Austrian Alpine provinces.

9, 10. Belt buckles, silver gilt. Herzegovina.

9A. Braid ornament. Dalmatia.

11, 12. Breast ornament, silver plate, gilded, set with stones, on strips of flannel. Dalmatia.

13. Hair ornament, silver gilt set with stones. Dalmatia.

(Museum für Österreichische Volkskunde, Vienna.)

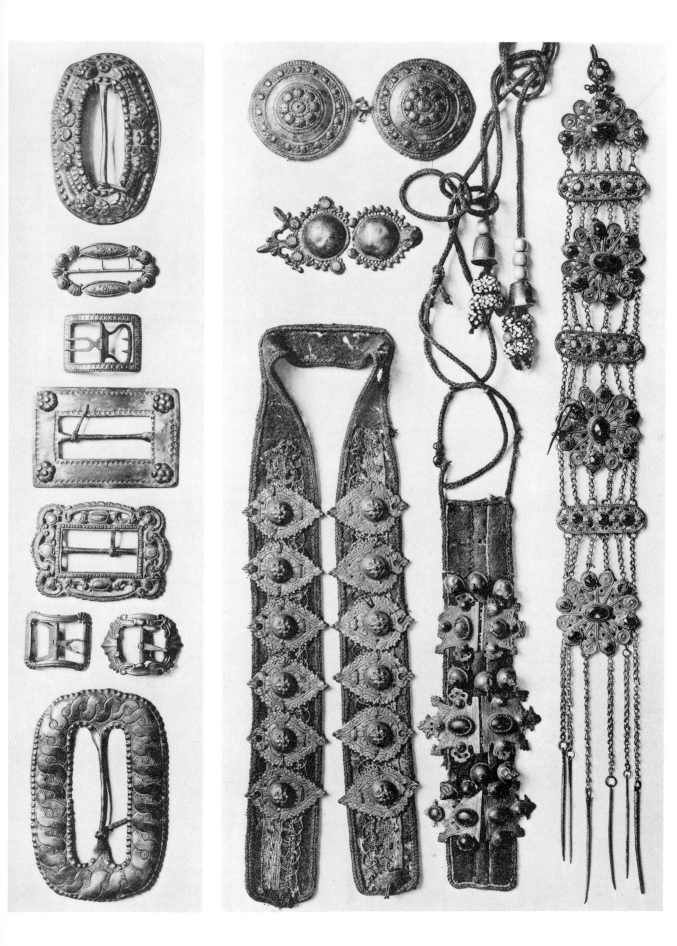

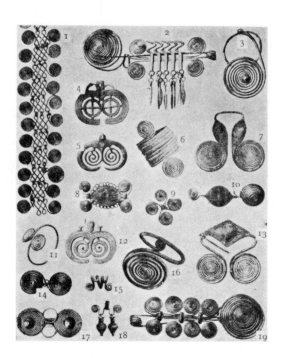

Plate 11

1. Bronze chain, 2000 B.C.
(Grossherzoglich Badische Sammlung für Altertümer und Völkerkunde, Karlsruhe.)

2. Bronze fibula with pendants, from the Mededze hoard, Komitat Árva, Hungary.

3. Spiral coil, bronze, from the (storage) find at Salgó-Tarjan, Hungary.

4, 5, 12. Bronze pendants. Hungary.
(National Museum, Budapest.)

6. Bronze arm bracelet, Bronze Age. Stockerau, Lower Austria.
(Naturhistorisches Museum, Vienna, Prehistorical Collection.)

7, 10, 13. Bronze fibulas. Klein-Hesebeck discovery site near Uetzen, Saxony.
(Grossherzoglich Badische Sammlung für Altertümer und Völkerkunde, Karlsruhe.)

8. Bronze fibula, fragment. Hungary.
(National Museum, Budapest.)

9, 14. Bronze fibulas, Hallstatt era. Hallstatt, Upper Austria.

11. Prehistoric bronze arm band. Galicia, Austria.
(Naturhistorisches Museum, Vienna, Prehistoric Collection.)

15. Bronze clasp ring, beginning of Iron Age. Caucasus.

16. Bronze arm band, Bronze Age. Stockerau, Lower Austria.

17. Bronze fibula, Hallstatt era. Propor near Otočac, Croatia.

18. Bronze pendant, Hallstatt era. Italy.

19. Bronze fibula, Bronze Age. Upper Hungary.
(Naturhistorisches Museum, Vienna, Prehistoric Collection.)

24

Plate 12

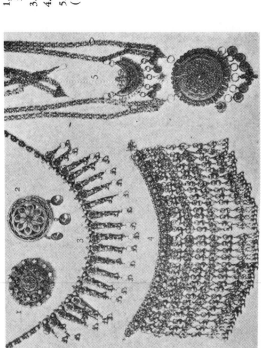

1, 2. Brooch, silver gilt, oxidized, imitation of Norwegian originals.
3. Necklace, oxidized silver, imitation of Arabic originals.
4. Breast ornament, oxidized silver, imitation of Arabic originals.
5. Pendant, oxidized silver, imitation of Arabic originals.
(Kunstgewerbliche Fachschule, Gablonz.)

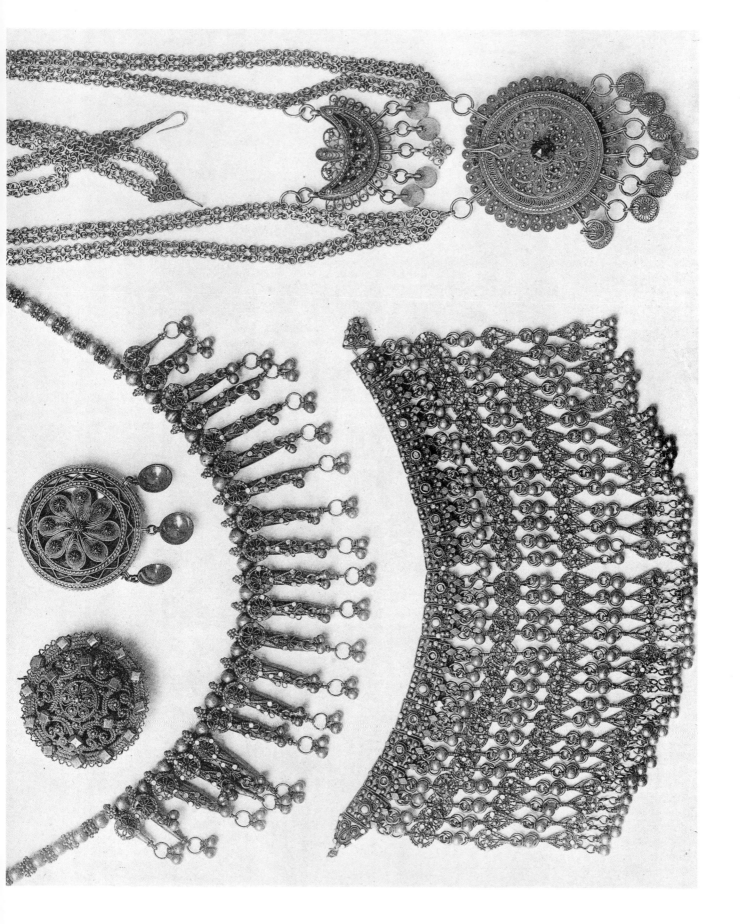

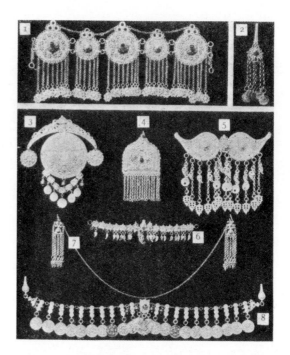

Plate 13

1. Silver necklace, partially gilded, adorned with lacquer colors and brightly colored stones. 18th to 19th century. Greece.

2. Silver hair pin, partially gilded, with red stone. 18th to 19th century. Greece.

3. Silver breast pendant, partially gilded, with red coral attachments. 19th century. Greece.

4. Breast ornament (part of a necklace), silver gilt and red stone. 19th century. Greece.

5. Silver cloak clasp. 19th century. Turkey.

6. Chain from a breast ornament, silver. 18th century. Greece.

7. Two earrings connected with silver chain, adorned with stones and coral. 18th century. Greece.

8. Silver breast pendant, partially gilded, adorned with stones and coral. 18th to 19th century. Greece.

(Kunstgewerbe-Museum, Berlin.)

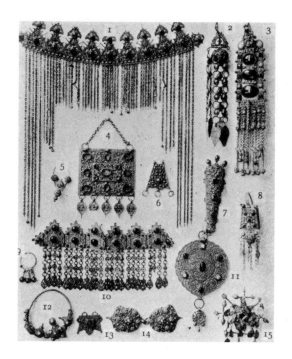

Plate 14

1. Diadem of yellow metal, adorned with beads and coral.
2. Earring of poor silver.
3. Silver gilt earring with coral and beads.
4. Breast pendant of yellow metal.
5. Earring.
6. Fragment of an earring; found with other jewelry in Erneszt-háza. 15th to 16th century.
7. Tuft-holder from a cap, silver gilt. Found in Bánostor.
8, 9. Earring of poor silver.
10. Diadem of poor silver.
11. Ornamental disc pendant of silver gilt, with carnelian and almandine decoration.
12. Earring decorated with beads and glass jewels, of poor silver.
13. Part of a hook and eye, poor silver.
14. Belt clasp, silver filigree work.
15. Silver breast hook. 14th to 15th century.
All objects south Slavic, chiefly from Serbia and Dalmatia.
(Ethnographic Division of the National Museum, Budapest.)

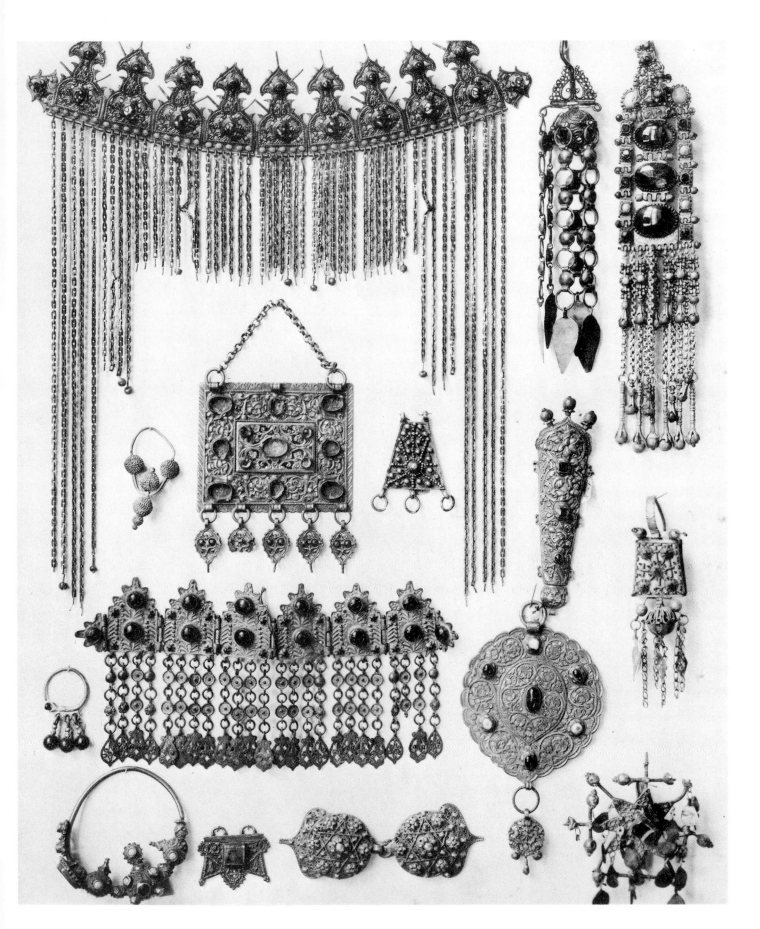

Plate 15

1. Button, silver with filigree. Lower German.

2, 4, 7, 9, 11, 12, 14, 21, 22, 25, 26, 27, 28, 32, 33, 34. All Russian peasant buttons.

3. Button with enamel. Transylvania.

5, 10. Button. Lower German.

6. Button. Lower Elbe.

8. Button. Vierlanden.

13. Rosary, gold, silver and pearls.

15. Button. Ukraine.

16. Button. Transylvania.

17. Button. North Germany (Hanover).

18. Button. Near Moscow.

19. Button.

20, 24. Lead buttons. Hungary.

23. Porcelain button. Meissen.

29, 31. Buttons.

30. Button with glass jewels. France.

35, 36. Buttons. Naples.

37. Button. Nuremberg.

38. Button. Klausenburg.

(Collection of Privy Councillor M. Rosenberg, Karlsruhe.)

Plate 16

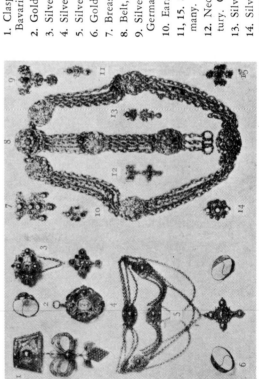

1. Clasp with pendant (grapes), peasant jewelry. 19th century. Bavaria (Upper Franconia).
2. Gold earring. Northern Germany.
3. Silver brooch. Salzburg.
4. Silver filigree pendant. Bavaria.
5. Silver necklace. Bavaria.
6. Gold earring. Northern Germany.
7. Breast ornament, silver with table-cut stones. Germany.
8. Belt, silver with gilded rosettes. Switzerland (Basel).
9. Silver neck ornament with emeralds and rubies. 18th century. Germany.
10. Earring of silver gilt with rubies. 18th century. Italy.
11, 15. Silver earrings with table-cut stones. 18th century. Germany.
12. Neck ornament with cross of silver with diamonds. 18th century. Germany.
13. Silver earring with diamonds. 18th century. Germany.
14. Silver neck ornament with Scottish pearls and garnets. 18th century. Germany.
(Germanisches Museum, Nuremberg.)

32

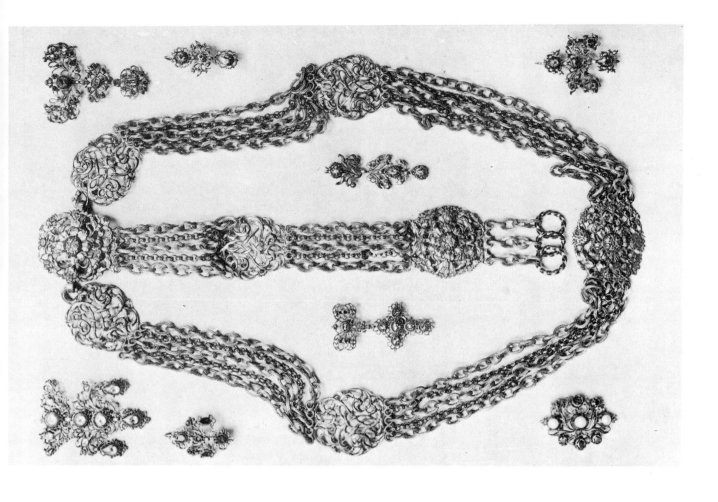

Plate 17

1. Woman's belt, silver gilt. Caucasus.
2, 9. Earrings, silver gilt. Caucasus.
3. Silver brooch. Caucasus.
4–6. Silver earrings. Caucasus.
7. Bronze ornament. Caucasus.
8. Half of a fibula. Caucasus.
10. Tin earring. Caucasus.
11. Silver pendant. Caucasus.
12, 13. Belt buckle, silver. Caucasus.
14. Burka clasp, silver. Caucasus.
15. Silver needle. Caucasus.
(Ethnographic Division of the National Museum, Budapest.)

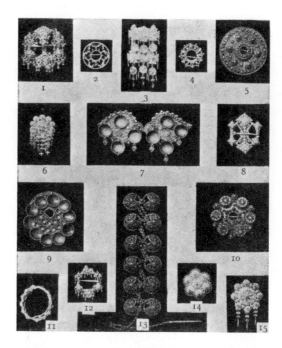

Plate 18

1. Buckle with double tongue, silver, partially gilded. 18th to 19th century. Norway.

2. Silver buckle, partially gilded. 17th century. Norway.

3. Silver brooch (work of A. A. Lie). 1878. Christiania [Oslo].

4. Silver buckle, partially gilded. 17th to 18th century. Norway.

5. Buckle (clothing clasp), silver, almost completely gilded. 19th century. Norway.

6. Silver brooch (work of Tostrupp). 1873. Norway.

7. Silver clasp in two parts, partially gilded. 18th century. Norway.

8. Silver buckle. 18th to 19th century. Norway.

9. Silver gilt buckle. 17th to 18th century. Norway.

10. Silver buckle, almost completely gilded. 18th century. Norway.

11. Arm band (work of Tostrupp). 1873. Christiania, Norway.

12. Silver buckle, partially gilded. 18th century. Norway.

13. Bib clasps with connecting chain, silver, partially gilded. 18th to 19th century. Norway.

14. Brooch (work of Tostrupp). 1872. Christiania, Norway.

15. Brooch (work of Tostrupp). 1871. Christiania, Norway.
(Kunstgewerbe-Museum, Berlin.)

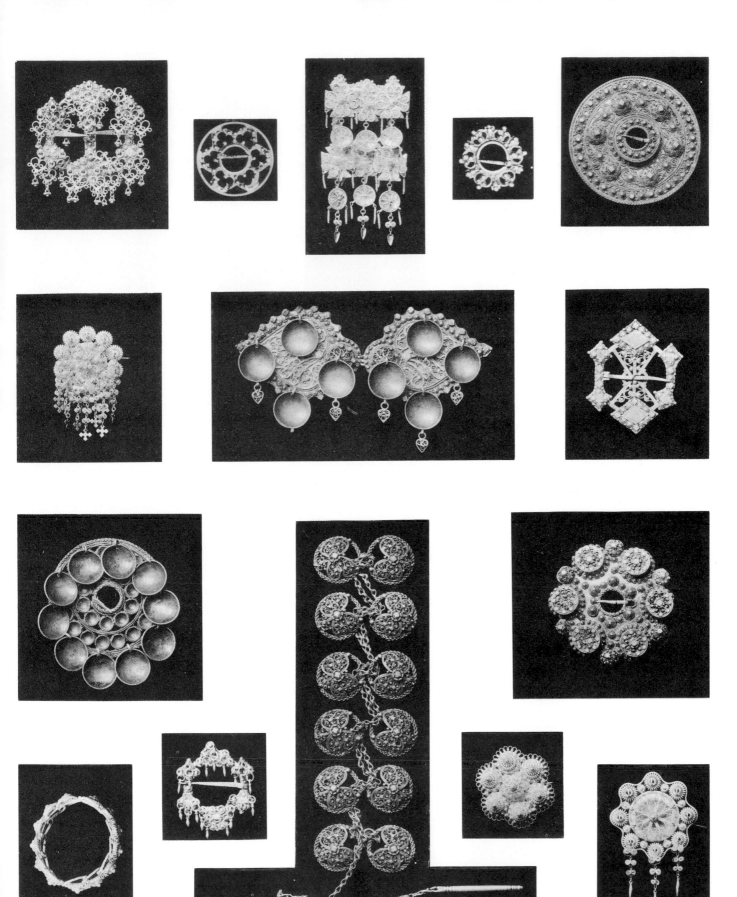

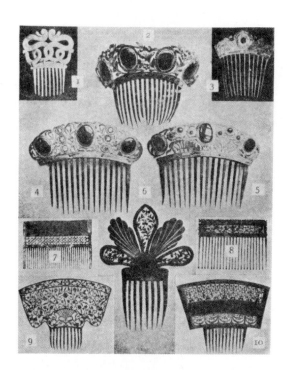

Plate 19

1. Horn comb. Austria.
(Museum für Österreichische Volkskunde, Vienna.)

2, 6. Horn comb. Upper Lusatia in Saxony.
(Museum für Völkerkunde, Dresden.)

3. Silver comb, filigree work with green and red stones. First half of 19th century. Warmbrunn in the Riesengebirge.
(Schlesisches Museum für Kunstgewerbe and Altertümer, Breslau.)

4, 5. Back combs, fire-gilt brass, with Bohemian carnelians and white crystal. Starkenbach, Northern Bohemia.
(Czechoslovakian Ethnographical Museum, Prague.)

7. Horn comb. Dated 1810. With open work. Silesia.

8. Horn combs with open work. Dated 1632. Silesia.
(Schlesisches Museum für Kunstgewerbe und Altertümer, Breslau.)

9, 10. Horn comb, pierced work.

Plate 20

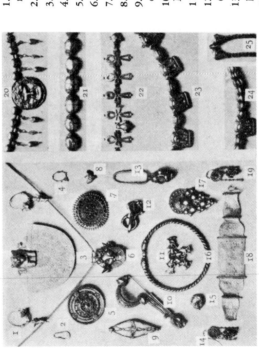

1. Earrings with genii and cornucopias, gold, after an ancient original. Italy.
2. Ancient gold earring. Italy.
3. Egyptian aegis, electrodeposit reproduction.
4. Gold earring, Etruscan. Italy.
5. Brooch from ancient original, enameled. Italy.
6. Bulla, copy of an Etruscan original from Cervetri, gold. Italy.
7. Round fibula from Caere, gold filigree, modern copy. Italy.
8. Winged head, gold, Etruscan. Italy.
9. Pendant ornament from the Vettersfelde gold hoard, electrodeposit reproduction. 6th century A.D. Italy.
10. Gold fibula, copy of ancient original in the Naples National Museum, Italy.
11. Gold belt ornament, East Gothic. 7th century A.D. Italy.
12. Buckle from the Petrossa hoard, electrodeposit reproduction. 6th century A.D. Italy.
13. Earring from the Vettersfelde hoard, gold, electrodeposit reproduction. Italy.
14. Gold earring with grapes, copy of ancient original. Italy.
15. Earring, gold with filigree, ancient. Italy.
16. Gold arm band, ancient. Italy.
17. Gold earring with grapes, copy of ancient original from Caere. Italy.
18. Electrum arm band, copy of an ancient original from Sardinia.
19. Gold earring with grapes, copy of an ancient original. Italy. (Österreichisches Museum für Kunst und Industrie, Vienna.)
20. Gold necklace. Etruria.
21-24. Gold necklaces. Ethiopia.
25. Gold necklace. Aegina, Greece. (Neue Pinakothek, Munich.)

40

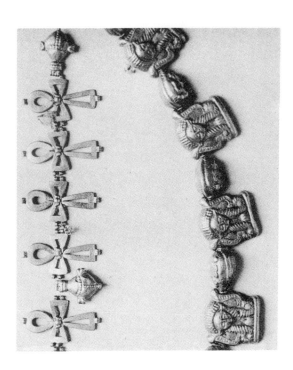

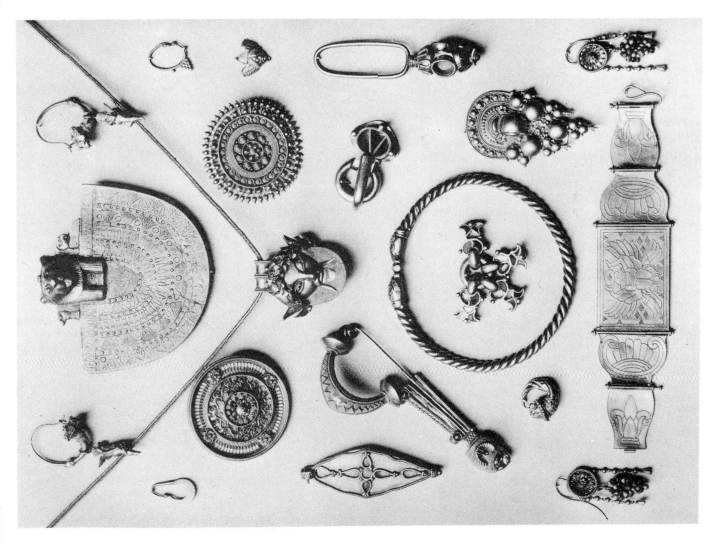

Plate 21

1, 18. Brass earrings. Sumatra.

2, 16, 17. Brass weights for gold dust (Ashanti), Africa. Guinea.

3. Man's earring, silver. Sunda Islands (Timor).
(Museum für Länder- und Völkerkunde, Stuttgart.)

4. Reliquary of gilded metal with colored enamel. Jaypur, India.

5. Amulet holder of gilded brass, set with turquoises. Sikkim, India.

6, 9. Silver amulet holders, set with turquoises. Sikkim, India.

7. Porcupine quill hair pin, mother of pearl above. Japan.

8. Hair pin of black bone, bronze above. Japan.

10. Metal hair pin with colored glass ball. Japan.

11. Brass comb. Sikkim, India.

12. Tortoise-shell comb with gold lacquer painting. Japan.

13, 15. Carved ivory combs. Japan.

14. Clothing ornament of silver, set with turquoises. Sikkim, India.
(Collection of Count Karl Lanckoroński, Vienna.)

Plate 22

2, 13. Jointed fibulas, older Hallstatt era. St. Lucia, Carniola.

3. Bow-shaped fibula, older Hallstatt era. St. Lucia, Carniola.

4. Half-moon fibula, older Hallstatt era. St. Lucia, Carniola.

5. Bow-shaped fibula, Hallstatt.

6. Hair pin. Bosnia.

7. Belt hook.

8. Snake-like fibula, later Hallstatt era.

9. Fibula in the shape of a horse. Bronze, later Hallstatt era.

10. Pendant. Hallstatt.

11. Wavy fibula, older Hallstatt era. St. Lucia, Carniola.

12, 27. Pendants. Bosnia.

14. Belt clasp. Koban (Caucasus).

15. Bronze fibula. Hallstatt.

16, 24. Part of a clasp. Koban (Caucasus).

17. Disc fibula. Hallstatt.

18. Ornament.

19. Boat-shaped fibula.

20. Ornament. Hallstatt.

21. Belt clasp. Koban (Caucasus).

22. Half-moon fibula. Hallstatt.

23. Pendant. Koban (Caucasus).

25. Bow-shaped fibula, older Hallstatt era. Watsch (Carniola).

26. Bow-shaped fibula, older Hallstatt era. Hallstatt.

All ornaments of bronze.

(Naturhistorisches Museum, Vienna, Prehistoric Collection.)

[NOTE: There is no number 1.]

Plate 23

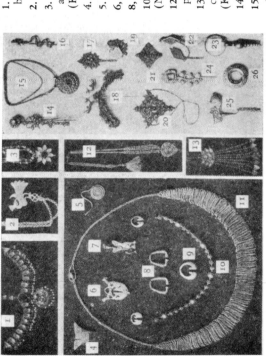

1. Forehead ornament. 1881. Brass with colorful glass inlay and beads. Benares, India.
2. Hook of a belt chain, silver with turquoises. Darjeeling, India.
3. Middle section of a necklace. Red silk cord with brass beads and glass inlay. 19th century. Bombay, India. (Kunstgewerbe-Museum, Berlin.)
4. Hair comb. Ceylon.
5. Ear ornament of the Igorots. Philippines.
6, 7. Gold amulets of the Igorots. Philippines.
8, 9. Gold ear ornaments of the Igorots. Philippines.
10, 11. Gold necklaces of the Igorots. Philippines. (Naturhistorisches Museum, Vienna, Ethnographic Collection.)
12. Necklace, red silk cord with brass beads and a pressed brass pendant. 19th century. Bombay, India.
13. Hair ornament, brass with colorfully inlaid bits of glass. 19th century. Bombay, India. (Kunstgewerbe-Museum, Berlin.)
14. Scarf pin, Suassa gold with glass jewelry. Java.
15. Medallion with chain, gold and glass jewels. Java.
16, 17. Scarf pins. Java.
18. Hair pin. Sumatra.
19. Neck ornament. Sumatra.
20, 21. Neck ornaments, Suassa gold with precious stones. Sumatra.
22. Scarf pin, gilded brass. Java.
23. Ear ornament. Sumatra.
24. Silver scarf pin. Java.
25. Neck ornament, gilded brass, pressed. Java.
26. Ring, pressed gold plate. (Naturhistorisches Museum, Vienna, Ethnographic Collection.)

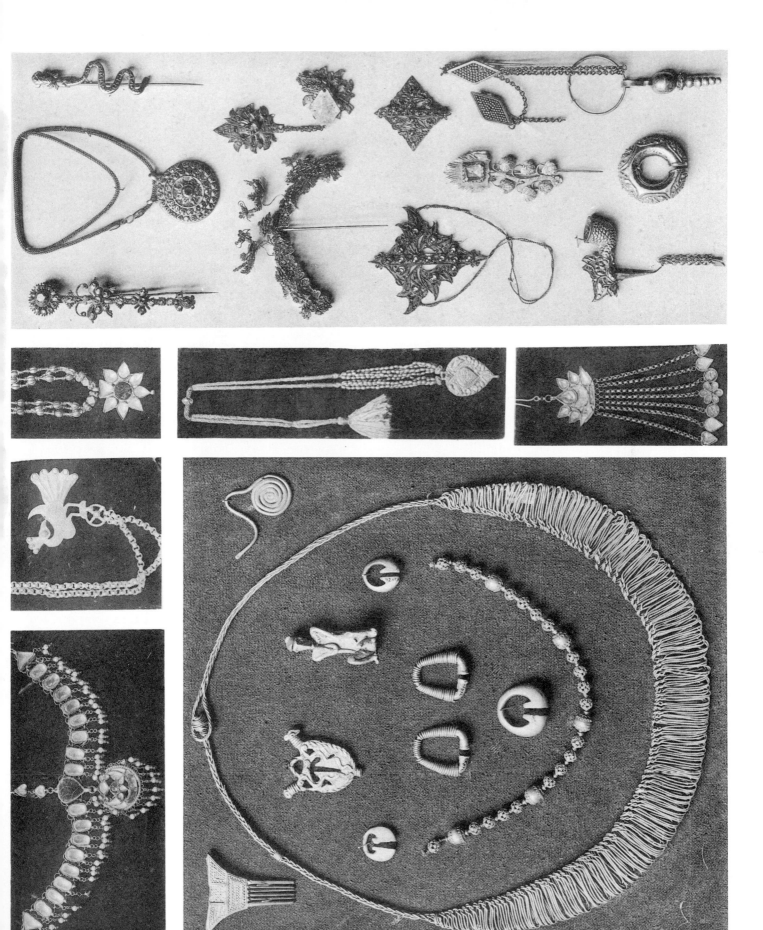

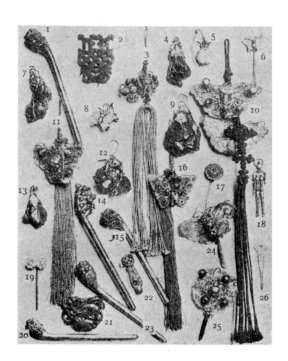

Plate 24

1, 14, 15, 20, 23. Silver hair pins. Korea.

2, 8, 21, 22, 26. Articles of jewelry. Korea.

3, 10, 11, 16. Fan ornaments, silver and mother of pearl. Korea.

4, 5, 7, 9, 12, 13. Pendants, silver with amber in the shape of fruits. Korea.

6, 17, 19. Pins. Korea.

18. Pendant. Korea.

24, 25. Ornamental catches, silver and mother of pearl. Korea.
(Museum für Völkerkunde, Leipzig.)

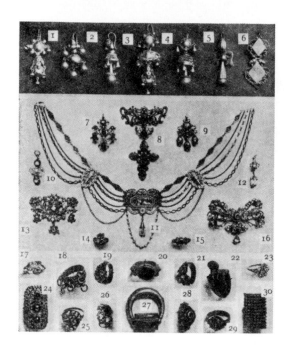

Plate 25

1–6. Earrings, silver. South Slavic.
(Österreichisches Museum für Kunst und Industrie, Vienna.)

7. Earring. 18th century. Germany.

8. Necklace cross. 18th century. Germany.

9. Earring. 18th century. Germany.

10. Earring. 17th century. Germany.

11. Necklace. Empire period. Germany.

12. Earring with Passau pearls. 17th century. Germany.
(Kunstgewerbe-Museum, Nuremberg.)

13. Brooch. 18th century. Germany.

14. Ring. 18th century. Germany.

15. Ring. 17th century. Germany.

16. Brooch. 17th century. Germany.
(Kunstgewerbe-Museum, Nuremberg.)

17. Ring with basket of flowers, silver gilt, modern work. Vienna.

18. Silver ring. Norway.

19. Ring with stones, silver gilt, modern work. Vienna.

20. Silver ring with stone with markings resembling writing.
Orient.

21. Ring with stones, silver gilt. Orient.

22. Ring with jackal's head. Vitreous paste. Egypt.

23. Ring with brilliants, modern work. Vienna.

24. Silver gilt ring with three glass jewels. Italy.

25. Silver gilt ring with turquoises. Italy.

26. Gold ring with four vitreous paste inlays, modern work.
Vienna.

27. Signet ring, electrodeposit reproduction. Egypt.

28. Silver gilt ring with two cherubs, with enamel and stones,
modern work. Vienna.

29, 30. Silver gilt rings. Italy.
(Österreichisches Museum für Kunst und Industrie, Vienna.)

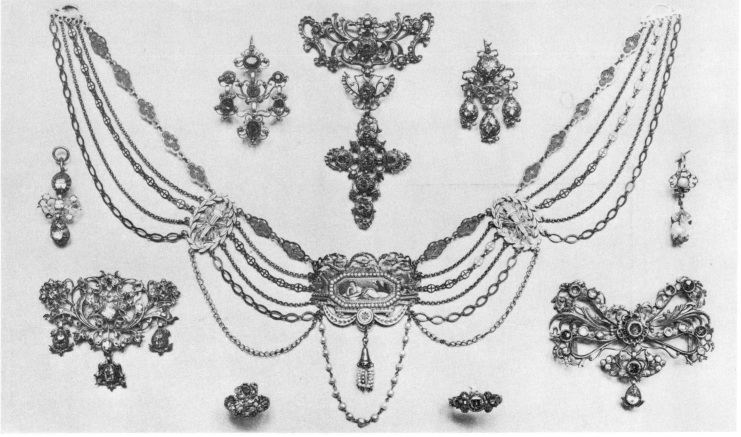

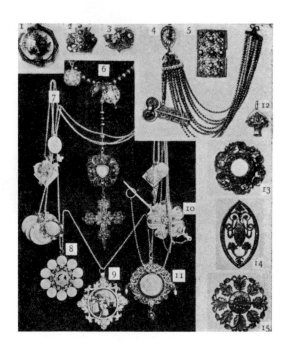

Plate 26

1. Pendant, gold filigree. End of the 18th century. Germany.
2. Silver filigree breast pin. Münsterland.
3. Silver filigree breast pin.
4. Silver watch chain. Salzburg.
5. Silver gilt neck clasp. 18th century. Bavaria.
6. Silver necklace. 18th century. Salzburg.

7–11. Large breast pendants with ornaments, silver. 18th century. Upper Bavaria.
(Formerly in the collection of the late Amalie Schönchen, actress of the Imperial Theater, Vienna.)

12. Pendant, silver gilt. 18th century. Upper Bavaria.
(Österreichisches Museum für Kunst und Industrie, Vienna.)

13–15. Brass ornaments. France.
(North Bohemian Commerce Museum, Reichenberg [Liberec], Bohemia.)

Plate 27

1, 2. Silver hair pins. Bulgaria (Sofia).

3. Necklace. Bulgaria (Sofia).

4. Earrings of bronze plate. Bulgaria (Sofia).

5. Necklace of yellowish metal. Bulgaria.

6. Earring of whitish alloy, "Küpe." Bulgaria (Trnova).

7. Hair ornament with little sheet-metal disks, the middle piece silver plate. Bulgaria (Zagora).

8. Earring, yellowish gray alloy. Bulgaria (Provadi).

9. Brass shoulder ornament. Bulgaria (Kotel).

10. Shoulder ornament of yellowish metal. Bulgaria (Kotel).

11. Silver arm band. Bulgaria (Kotel).

12. Forehead ornament of yellow metal with Turkish silver coins. Bulgaria (Zagora). (Naturhistorisches Museum, Vienna, Ethnographic Collection.)

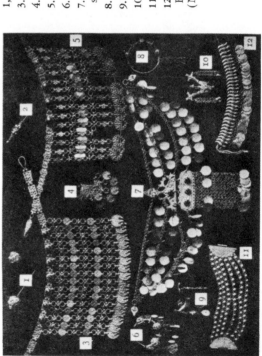

54

Plate 28

1. Earring, gilded silver filigree. 19th century. Syria.
2. Gold necklace with 8 pieces and 2 knobs. 19th century. Timbuctoo.
3, 13. Silver earrings with enamel. 19th century. Oriental.
4. Gold arm band with filigree. 19th century. Timbuctoo.
5. Silver earrings with enamel. 19th century. Oriental.
6. Gold necklace of 8 pieces and 2 knobs. 19th century. Timbuctoo.
7–9. Clasps. 19th century. Lycia.
10. Gold frog. Precolumbian civilization. Colombia.
11. Woman's ear ornament, metal filigree. Malayan.
12. Silver brooch with turquoises. Syria.
14. Earring made from gold coins. 19th century. Turkey.
15. Silver chain ornament, with beads. 19th century. Syria.
16. Silver brooch with turquoises and red stones. 19th century. Syria.
17. Half-moon-shaped brooch, silver filigree. 19th century. Syria.
18, 20. Silver filigree arm band. 19th century. South Arabia.
19. Silver forehead ornament. 19th century. South Arabia.
(Österreichisches Museum für Kunst und Industrie, Vienna.)

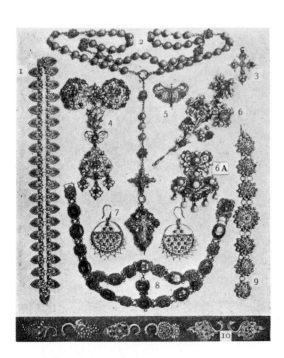

Plate 29

1. Silver necklace. Saxony.
2. Rosary of alabaster beads with silver filigree pendant. Switzer·
land.
3. Small gold cross. Germany.
4. Silver pendant. Southern Germany.
5. Pendant. Southern Germany.
6. Brooch. Southern Germany.
6A. Silver pendant. 19th century. Southern Germany.
7. Silver gilt earrings.
8. Silver gilt necklace. Southern Germany.
9. Silver arm band.
(Kunstgewerbe-Museum, Dresden.)
10. Silver bodice catches. Augsburg and Munich work, 1750–1830.
(Owner: Theodor Heiden, court jeweler, Munich.)

Plate 30

1, 5, 11, 12. Blouse clasps, silver filigree on a gilded foil. Vierlanden.

2, 3. Blouse pins, silver filigree with glass-covered pictures, garnet rosette on a gilded foil. Vierlanden.

4. Blouse pin, silver filigree with garnets on a gilded foil. Vierlanden.

6, 8, 14, 17. Blouse pins, silver filigree with 4 garnets on a gilded foil. Vierlanden.

7. Silver gilt earrings. Vierlanden.

9. Silver "Bossen" (bosom) on a gold-embroidered bodice; above, a blouse pin in gilded silver filigree work with a rosette of blue vitreous paste. From the "Altes Land" on the Elbe, Hanover Province.

10. Breast chain, the two side pieces silver gilt, the links silver, the middle section silver filigree on a gilded foil. Vierlanden.

13. Silver gilt earrings. Vierlanden.

15, 16. Blouse pins, silver filigree with 4 glass-covered mounted flower pictures on a gilded foil. Vierlanden.

18. Blouse pin, silver filigree with 6 blue-green stones (vitreous paste) on a gilded foil. Vierlanden.
(Museum für Kunst und Gewerbe, Hamburg.)

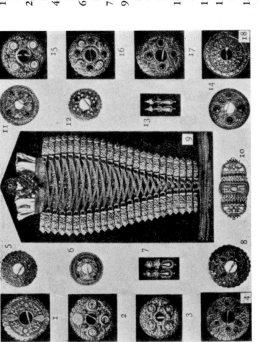

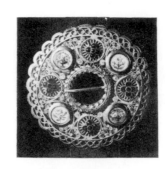

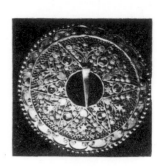

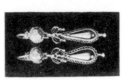

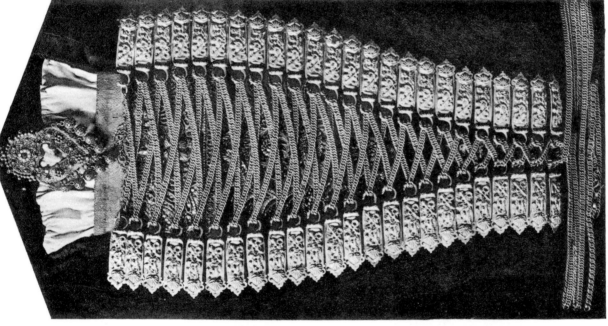

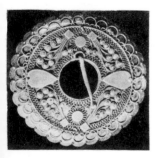
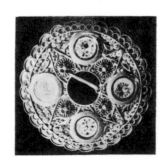

Plate 31

1. Glass medallion with silhouette, in silver gilt mount (Nuremberg workmanship). Nuremberg.
(Collection of A. Merklein, goldsmith, Nuremberg.)

2. Gold pendant with ivory miniature, Empire.

3. Gilded copper pendant, Empire.

4. Gold pendant with ivory, Empire. Austria.

5. Gold enamel hunting whistle. 16th century. Germany.

7. Gold enamel pendant. Beginning of 19th century. Geneva.

8. Gold pendant with enamel, neo-rococo, 1830. Southern Germany.

9. Gold pendant with enamel. The inscription reads "Vergiss mein nicht" (forget me not); the "3" (*drei*) inscribed on the heart is a visual pun for *treu* (faithful). 17th century. Southern Germany.

10. Silver gilt pendant, wth a "3" on the heart. 17th century. Southern Germany.

11. Gold pendant, Empire.

12. Gold pendant with black enamel. Emblems with corresponding inscription. 16th century.

13. Gold chain, Empire.

14. Gold ring with precious stones. Persia.
(Collection of Privy Councillor M. Rosenberg, Karlsruhe.)

15–19. So-called *Paten- und Dukatenbüchslein* (godfather-and-ducat boxes), silver (Nuremberg workmanship). Nuremberg.
(Collection of A. Merklein, goldsmith, Nuremberg.)

[NOTE: There is no number 6.]

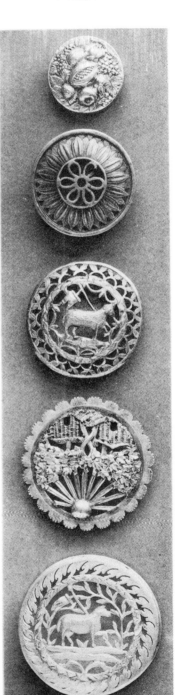

Plate 32

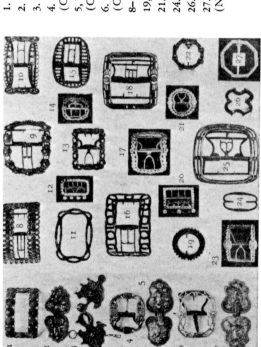

1. Silvered shoe buckle. East Frisia.
2. Silver cloak buckle. Westphalia.
3. Bronze cloak buckle. Lindau am Bodensee.
4. Bronze shoe buckle. Württemberg.
   (Collection of C. Esslinger, Postal Director, Leer.)
5, 7. Silver cloak buckles. Cologne.
   (Collection of Friedrich Laue, Cologne.)
6. Silver shoe buckle. East Frisia.
   (Collection of C. Esslinger, Postal Director, Leer.)
8–18, 20, 23, 25. Shoe buckles. 17th to 18th century. England.
19, 22. Brooches. 17th to 18th century. England.
21. Belt buckle. 17th to 18th century. England.
24. Belt buckle. 19th century. England.
26. Shoe buckle. 19th century. England.
27. Silver brooch. England.
   (National Museum, Edinburgh.)

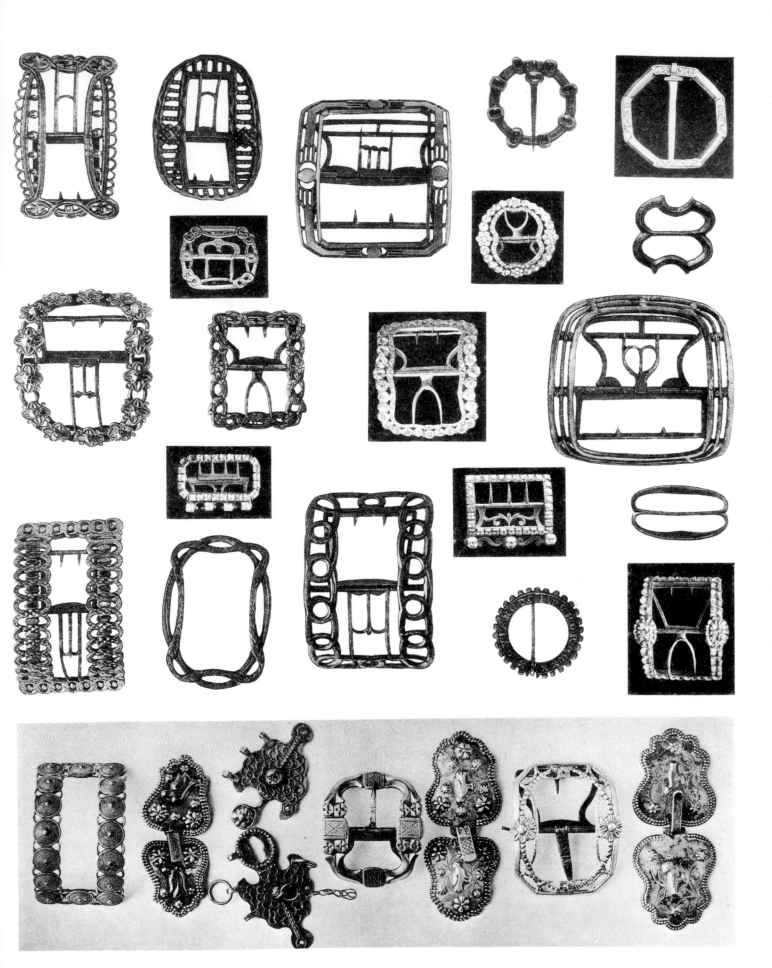

Plate 33

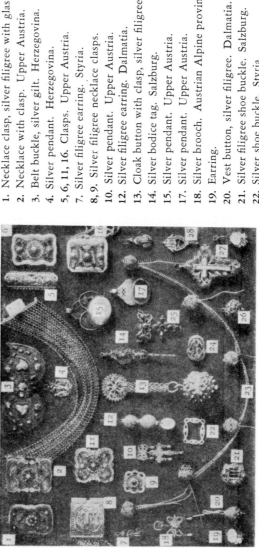

1. Necklace clasp, silver filigree with glass jewels. Upper Austria.
2. Necklace with clasp. Upper Austria.
3. Belt buckle, silver gilt. Herzegovina.
4. Silver pendant. Herzegovina.
5, 6, 11, 16. Clasps. Upper Austria.
7. Silver filigree earring. Styria.
8, 9. Silver filigree necklace clasps.
10. Silver pendant. Upper Austria.
12. Silver filigree earring. Dalmatia.
13. Cloak button with clasp, silver filigree. Dalmatia.
14. Silver bodice tag. Salzburg.
15. Silver pendant. Upper Austria.
17. Silver pendant. Upper Austria.
18. Silver brooch. Austrian Alpine provinces.
19. Earring.
20. Vest button, silver filigree. Dalmatia.
21. Silver filigree shoe buckle. Salzburg.
22. Silver shoe buckle. Styria.
23. Silver filigree bodice pins with chain. Salzburg.
24. Silver filigree brooch. Styria.
25. Pendant. Upper Austria.
26. Silver filigree vest button. Dalmatia.
27. Rosary pendant, silver filigree with enamel. Salzburg.
28. Blouse clasp, silver. Silesia.
(Museum für Österreichische Volkskunde, Vienna.)

66

Plate 34

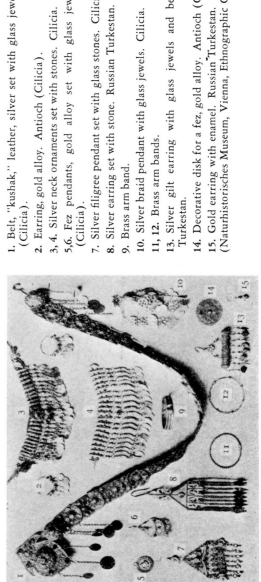

1. Belt, "kushak," leather, silver set with glass jewels. Saryawak (Cilicia).
2. Earring, gold alloy. Antioch (Cilicia).
3, 4. Silver neck ornaments set with stones. Cilicia.
5,6. Fez pendants, gold alloy set with glass jewels. Antioch (Cilicia).
7. Silver filigree pendant set with glass stones. Cilicia.
8. Silver earring set with stone. Russian Turkestan.
9. Brass arm band.
10. Silver braid pendant with glass jewels. Cilicia.
11, 12. Brass arm bands.
13. Silver gilt earring with glass jewels and beads. Russian Turkestan.
14. Decorative disk for a fez, gold alloy. Antioch (Cilicia).
15. Gold earring with enamel. Russian Turkestan. (Naturhistorisches Museum, Vienna, Ethnographic Collection.)

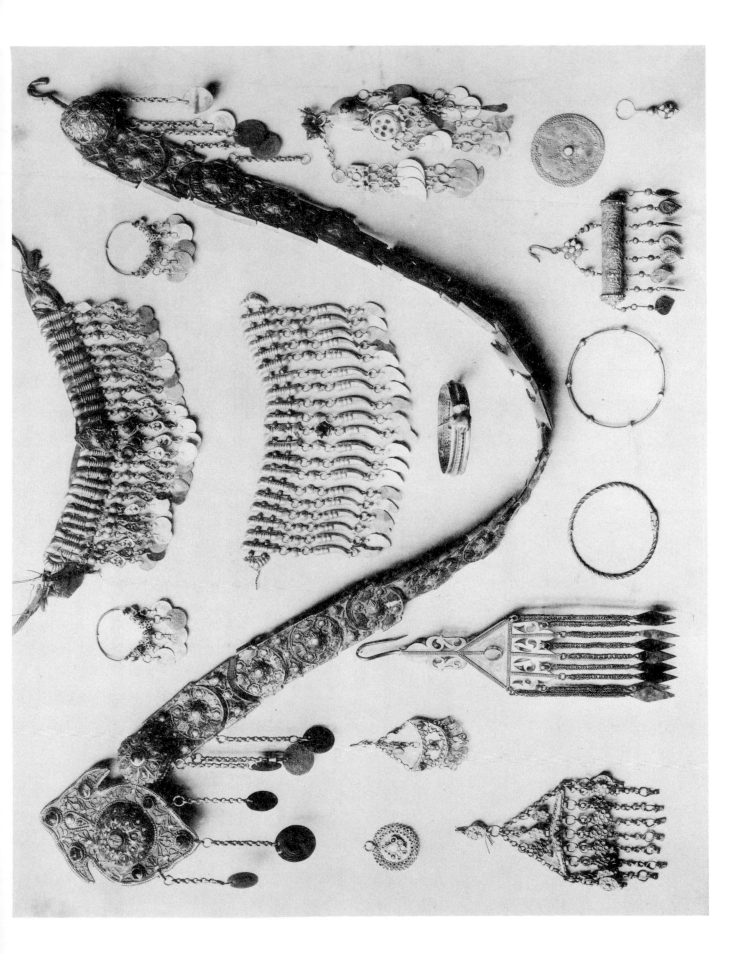

Plate 35

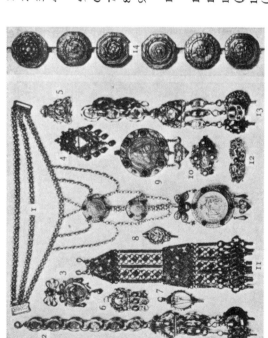

1. Silver bodice ornament. Vienna, around 1850. Lower Austria.
2. Silver watch chain. 18th century. Upper Bavaria.
3. Silver gilt pendant. 18th century. Bavaria.
4. Silver breast pin with turquoises and garnets. Regional jewelry. 18th century. Holstein.
5. Silver chain link. 18th century. Upper Bavaria.
6. Link from a silver watch chain. 18th century. Upper Bavaria.
7. Silver watch key. 18th century. Upper Bavaria.
8. Silver watch key. 18th century. Germany.
9. Medal of 1709 mounted in silver filigree with stones. Low German workmanship. Germany.
10. Silver filigree breast ornament. Münsterland workmanship of the 18th century.
11. Silver watch chain. 18th century. Norway.
12. Silver belt clasp. 18th century. Germany.
13. Silver watch chain. 18th century. Upper Bavaria. (Österreichisches Museum für Kunst und Industrie, Vienna.)
14. Brass buttons. Neighborhood of Karlsbad. (Owner: Theodor Heiden, court jeweler, Munich.)

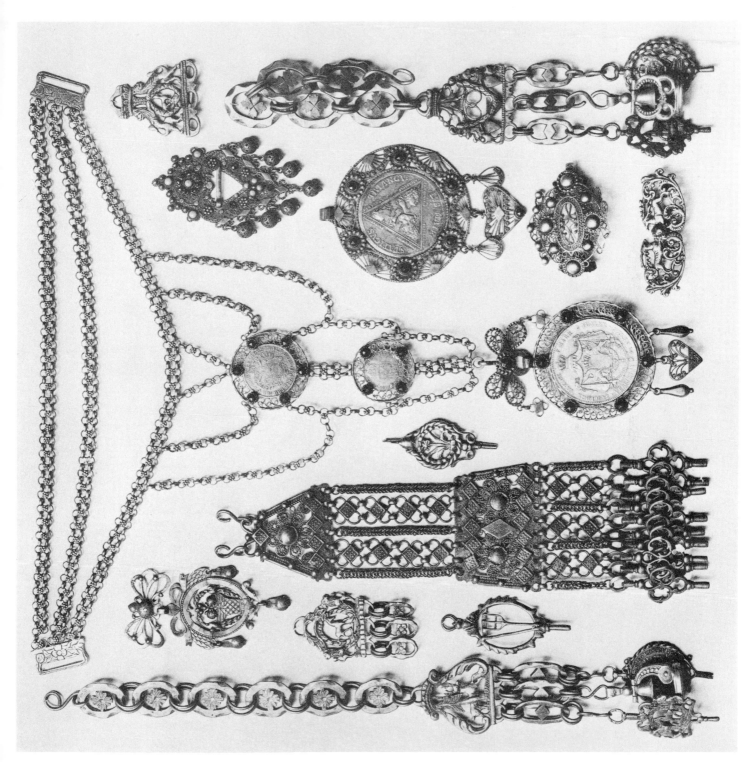

Plate 36

1. Wooden comb bound with bast. Samoa.

2, 3, 5, 8, 9, 15, 17. Wooden combs. Anchorite Islands.
(Museum für Länder- und Völkerkunde, Stuttgart.)

4. Horn comb. 19th century. England.
(British Museum, London.)

6. Wooden comb. Hermit Islands.

7, 11, 13. Wooden comb. Samoa.
(Museum für Länder- und Völkerkunde, Stuttgart.)

10. Ivory comb. 16th century. England.
(British Museum, London.)

12. Wooden comb. Ninigo Island.
(Museum für Länder- und Völkerkunde, Stuttgart.)

14. Tortoise-shell comb with silver, "piqué" work. 18th century.
England.

16. Tortoise-shell comb. 17th century. England.

18. Tortoise-shell comb. Beginning of the 19th century. England.
(British Museum, London.)

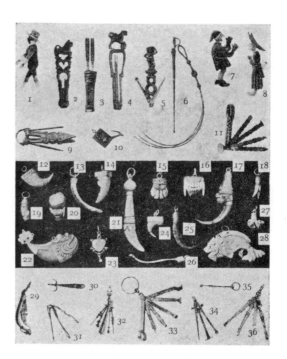

Plate 37

1. Toothpick of gray horn with ivory.

2, 4, 5. Ivory toothpicks. 18th to 19th century.

3. Toothpick consisting of knife and fork, in leather case with brass covering. 18th to 19th century. Worms.

6. Toothpick and ear pick, the latter of iron, the former of animal matter, bound in gold wire. 18th century. Silesia.

7, 8. Toothpicks of black horn and ivory, movable limbs. 19th century.

9. Toothpick and tweezers, copper. 18th to 19th century. Cairo.

10. Fingernail cleaner of damascened iron. Time of Louis XVI.

11. Toothpick, ear pick and signet with caryatids, around 1600.

12, 22, 28. Pendants, tiger claws, hunting trophies.

13, 15, 18, 19, 24, 26, 27. Pendants, hunting trophies.

14. Pendant, lobster claw, hunting trophy.

16, 20. Pendants, beaver mouths, hunting trophies.

17, 25. Pendants, bird talons, hunting trophies.

21. Children's pendant.

23. Pendant, deer teeth, hunting trophies.

29. Toothpick in the shape of a knife. 16th century. Switzerland.

30. Napkin holder, to be placed in the collar, silver, enamel. 18th century.

31, 32, 33, 36. Toothpicks. 17th to 18th century.

34. Toothpick, ear pick and signet. 19th century.

35. Ear pick. 18th century.

(Collection of Privy Councillor M. Rosenberg, Karlsruhe.)

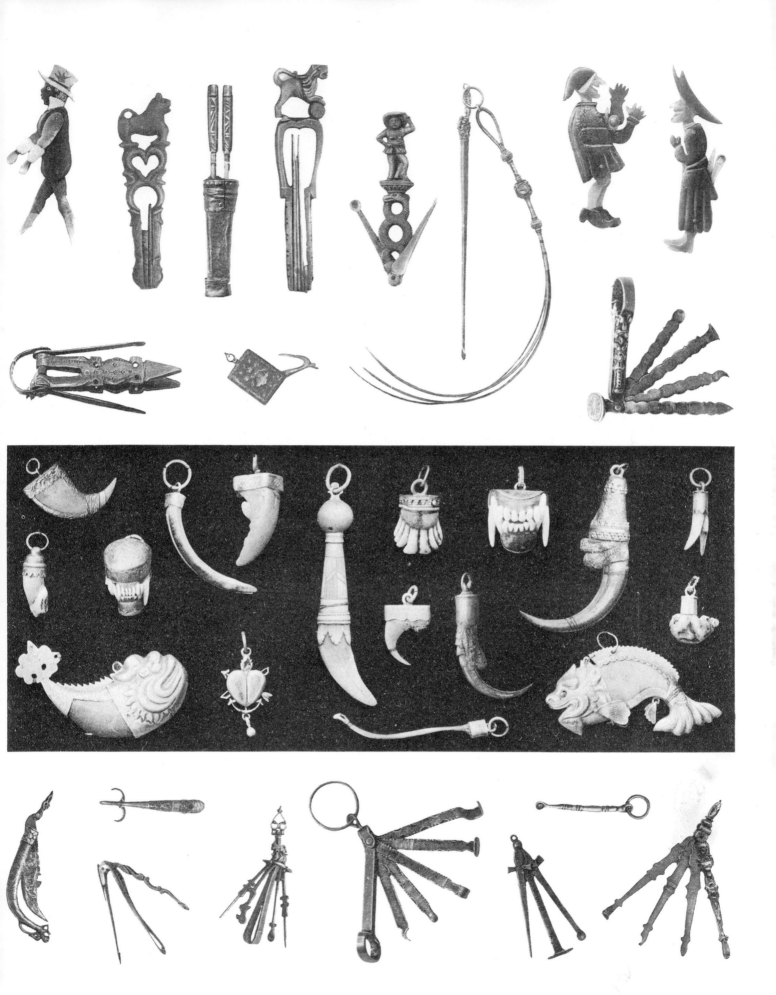

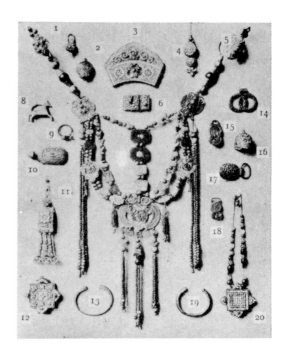

Plate 38

1. Brass ornament. From Yarkand, Chinese Turkestan.
2. Malachite pendant with silver filigree. Yarkand.
3. Silver filigree ornament set with turquoises. Ladak.
4. Earring, gilded and set with turquoises. Ladak.
5. Breast pendant.
6. Ornament. Yarkand.
8. Brass clasp. Yarkand.
9. Gilded earring, set with turquoises. Ladak.
10. Brass clasp with hook. Yarkand.
11. Pendant. Ladak.
12. Amulet holder, gilded and set with turquoises. Ladak.
13. Brass arm band. Ladak.
14. Buckle. Yarkand.
15. Small clasp. Yarkand.
16. Ornament. Mongolia.
17. Buckle. Yarkand.
18. Small clasp. Yarkand.
19. Arm band. Ladak.
20. Amulet holder with neck band set with turquoises. Ladak.
(Naturhistorisches Museum, Vienna, Ethnographical Collection.)
[NOTE: There is no number 7.]

Plate 39

1, 2, 4, 5. Bronze brooches. Anglo-Saxon.
(British Museum, London.)

3. Silver brooch with white stones. Anglo-Saxon.
(National Museum, Edinburgh.)

6. Bronze filigree brooch. Anglo-Saxon.

7, 8, 10, 11, 12, 14, 15, 16. Silver brooches. Anglo-Saxon.

9. Silver brooch with precious gems. Anglo-Saxon.

13. Bronze brooch. Anglo-Saxon.
(National Museum, Edinburgh.)

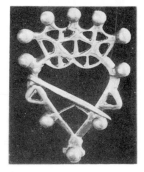

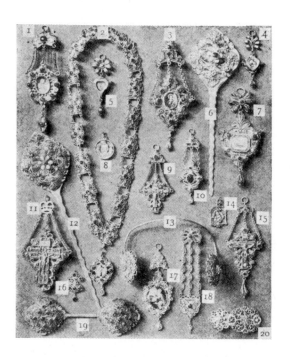

Plate 40

1. Rosary pendant with eglomisé (inner gilding). Canton Aargau, Switzerland.
2. Silver filigree belt chain. Freiamt, Canton Aargau, Switzerland.
3, 4. Rosary pendants with eglomisé. Canton Aargau, Switzerland.
5. Pendant.
6. Silver filigree hair pin. Nidwalden, Switzerland.
7. Enameled pendant. Canton Lucerne, Switzerland.
8. Pendant. Central Switzerland.
9, 10. Silver filigree pendants for rosaries. Canton Aargau, Switzerland.
11. Rosary pendant. (Lucerne?) Central Switzerland.
12. Hair pin, enamel and silver gilt. Nidwalden, Switzerland.
13. Silver filigree head ornament. Engadin, Switzerland.
14. Silver pendant. Central Switzerland.
15. Rosary pendant. Central Switzerland.
16. Pendant. Central Switzerland.
17. Pendant with eglomisé. Central Switzerland.
18. Breast-chain pendant, always worn in pairs. Klein-Appenzell, Switzerland.
19. "Rose pin," hair pin for unmarried girl. Canton Schwyz, Switzerland.
20. Chain link. Central Switzerland.
(Landes-Museum, Zurich.)

Plate 41

1. Silver earrings. Caucasus.

2. Silver filigree earring. Caucasus.

3. Silver filigree clasp. Caucasus.

4. Silver filigree brooch. Caucasus.

5. Silver filigree earrings. Caucasus.

6. Silver filigree clasp. Caucasus.
(Ethnographic Division of the National Museum, Budapest.)

7. Silver pendant, gilded and set with stones. 18th to 19th century. Bavaria.

8. Breast ornament, gold filigree with pearls. 17th to 18th century. Venice.
(Kunstgewerbe-Museum, Berlin.)

9. Gold earring, modern workmanship. Egypt.

10. Necklace of little rods, modern workmanship. Egypt.

11. Gilded metal breast ornament. Serbia.

12. Silver arm band, turned, modern workmanship. Egypt.

13. Brooch-earring with tiger claw, gold. China.

14. Silver arm band with bells, modern workmanship. Egypt.

15. Breast ornament with tiger claw, gold filigree. China.

16. Silver filigree arm band with bells, modern workmanship. Egypt.

17. Silver arm band with knobs, modern workmanship. Egypt.

18. Silver horse ornament. Serbia.

19. Silver arm ring with 2 knobs, modern workmanship. Egypt.
(Österreichisches Museum für Kunst und Industrie, Vienna.)

Plate 42

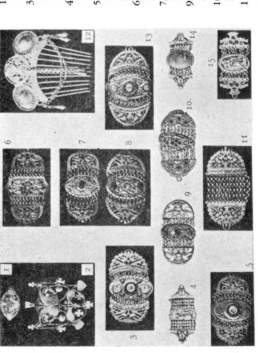

1, 2. Pendant with chain clasp, silver gilt, from Choppenburg. Saterland.

3, 13. Breast chains, the middle piece of silver filigree with garnets and partial gilding, 3 glass-covered painted pictures in round smooth frames; the two side pieces of silver gilt. Vierlanden.

4, 14. Breast chains, middle piece and side pieces silver gilt, links of silver. Vierlanden.

5. Breast chain, middle piece and side pieces silver gilt, silver links and central ornament of silver filigree with garnet rosettes and glass-covered painted picture. Vierlanden.

6. Breast chain, middle piece and combining links silver, the two side pieces silver gilt set with garnets. Vierlanden.

7, 8. Breast chains, middle piece and links of silver, silver gilt right and left, set with garnets. Vierlanden.

9. Breast chain, silver gilt in the middle piece with 3 mounted stones. Vierlanden.

10. Breast chain, foils of silver gilt, links and upper layers silver filigree set with garnets. Vierlanden.

11. Breast chain, side pieces of silver gilt, links of silver. Vierlanden.

12. Silver hair comb. East Frisia.

15. Breast chain, side pieces and middle piece of silver gilt, central overlay and links of silver. Vierlanden.
(Museum für Kunst und Gewerbe, Hamburg.)

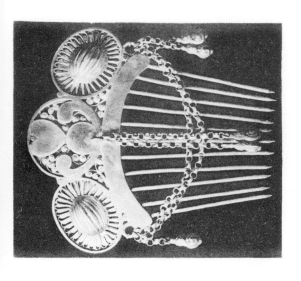

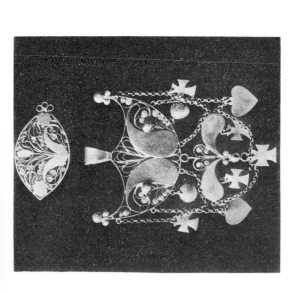

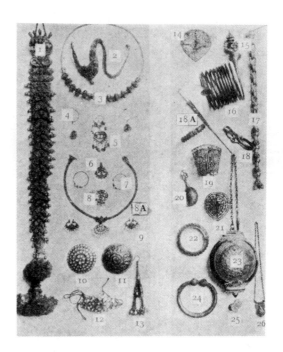

Plate 43

1. Braid ornament. Southern India.
2. Arm band. Southern India.
3. Neck band. Southern India.
4–9. Nose rings. Southern India.
8A. Neck ornament. Southern India.
10, 11. Disks worn on top of the head. Southern India.
12. Neck ornament. Southern India.
13. Ear ornament. India.
14. Amulet. India.
15. Thumb ring. India.
16. Arm band. India (Assam).
17. Foot chain. India.
18, 22. Arm bands. Ceylon.
18A. Hair pin. Ceylon.
19. Amulet. India.
20. Perfume container. Kashmir.
21. Stamp for ash decorations. India.
23. Lime box. Ceylon.
24. Arm band. Siam.
25. Ring. Ceylon.
26. Pubic covering. Indo-China.
(Naturhistorisches Museum, Vienna, Ethnographic Collection.)

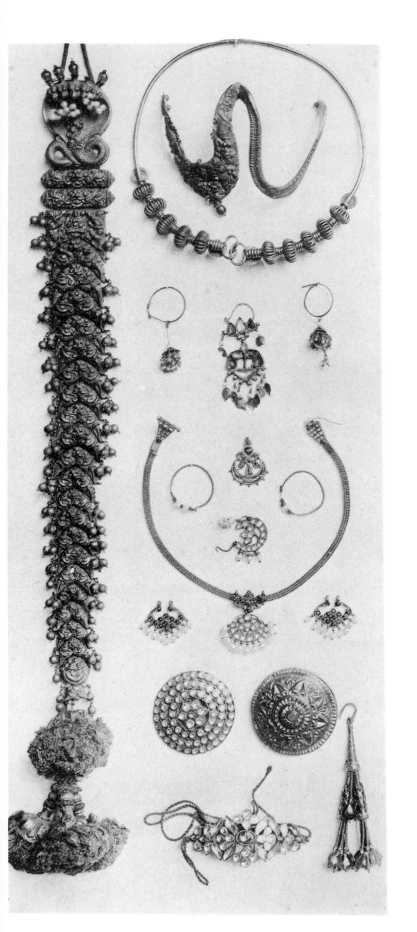
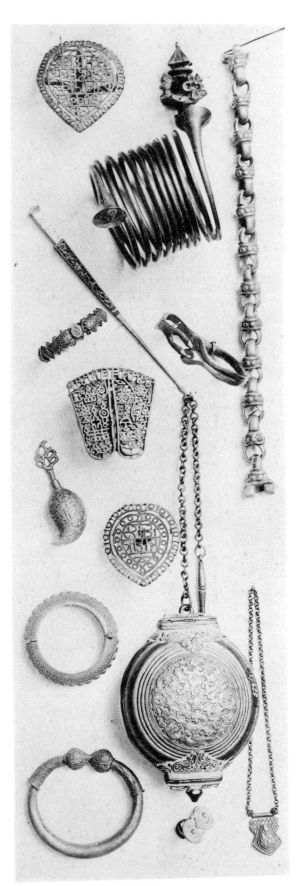

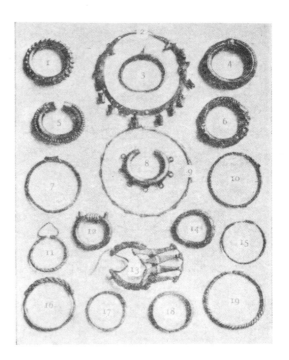

Plate 44

1. Arm band of the Djurr tribe. Upper White Nile region.
2. Neck band of the Bari tribe. Africa.
3. Upper-arm band of the Kich tribe. Africa.
4, 5. Wrist bands of the Djurr tribe. Upper White Nile region.
6. Wrist band of the Bateke. Africa.
7. Arm band. Benin. Africa.
8. Wrist band of the Djurr tribe. Africa.
9. Neck band of the Madi. Upper White Nile region.
10. Arm band. Benin. Africa.
11. Wrist ring of the Madi. Africa.
12. Arm band. Upper White Nile region.
13. Leather arm band. Galla. East Africa.
14. Arm band. Equatorial West Africa.
15. Arm band. West Africa.
16–18. Arm bands. Benin. Africa.
19. Arm band of the Madi. Africa.
(Naturhistorisches Museum, Vienna, Ethnographic Collection.)

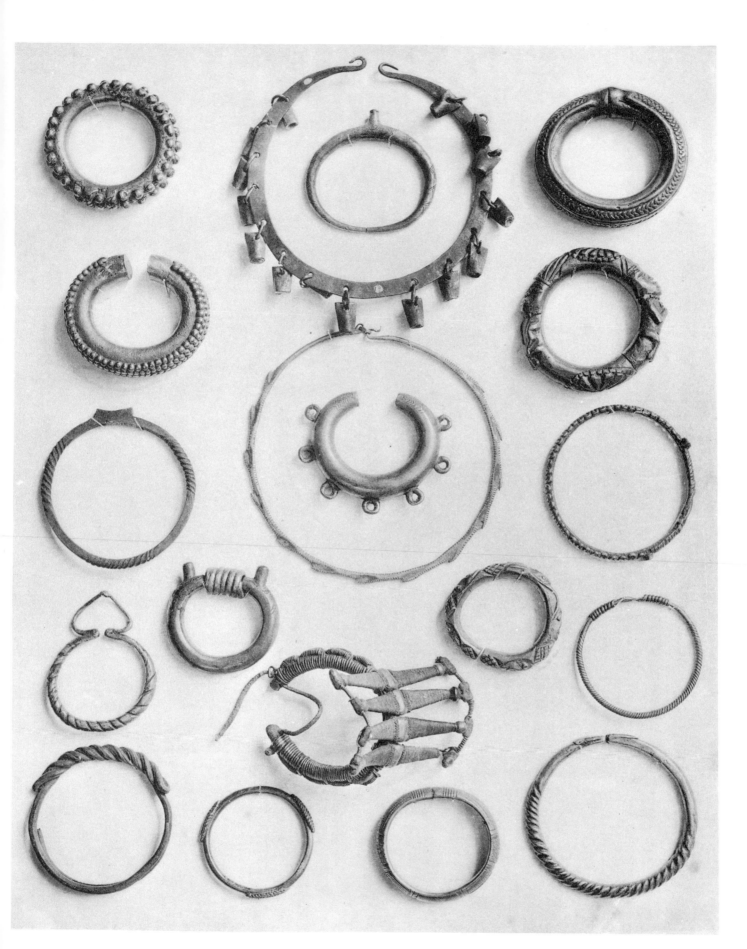

Plate 45

1. Silver gilt forehead chain with stones. East Frisia.
2. Golden belt buckle with silver chain and black band. East Frisia (Leer).
3. Silver gilt pendant (*Krüzbengel,* "clapper cross"). Saterland (Sögel).
4. Gold filigree clasp in three parts, with silver chain. East Frisia (Leer).
5. Earring. East Frisia (Nortenoon).
6, 7. Two golden earrings. East Frisia (Bingum and Goltland).
8. Golden tie pin. East Frisia (Filsum).
9. Gold filigree clasp in one part. East Frisia (Riepe).
10. Gold ring. East Frisia (Nortenoor).
11. Gold filigree clasp in one part, with silver chain. East Frisia (Oldersum).
12. Gold ring. East Frisia (Leer).
13. Gold pendant (*Krüzbengel*). Saterland (Quakenbrück).
14. Gold ring. East Frisia (Emden).
15. Gold filigree clasp (so-called "crown clasp") with silver chain. East Frisia (Aurich).
16. Gold belt clasp in two parts. East Frisia (Goltland).
17. Gold filigree earring. East Frisia (Leer).
18. Filigree clasp in three parts, with silver chain. East Frisia (Bagband).
19. Gold tie pin. East Frisia (Stickelband).
20. Filigree clasp in one part. East Frisia (Bagband).
21. Gold filigree earring. East Frisia (Dornum).
22. Gold filigree clasp in one part. East Frisia (Filsum).
(Collection of C. Esslinger, Postal Director, Leer, East Frisia.)

Plate 46

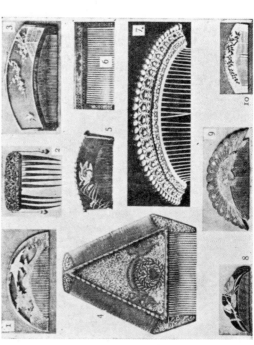

1. Ornamental ivory comb, tinted red, with gold decorations and flying crane in natural-colored ivory. Japan. (Museum für Kunst und Gewerbe, Hamburg.)

2. Horn comb with enameled pierced silver overlays. 18th century. (Gewerbe-Museum, Bremen.)

3. Ornamental comb of tortoise-shell with engraved glass pane. Japan. (Museum für Kunst und Gewerbe, Hamburg.)

4. Horn comb, partially painted and gilded. Vierlanden. (Gewerbe-Museum, Bremen.)

5. Ornamental comb of tortoise-shell with silver mount, decorated with gold lacquer, the natural-colored sparrows in lacquer relief. Japan. (Museum für Kunst und Gewerbe, Hamburg.)

6. Horn comb. Vierlanden.

7. Diadem comb with coral beads. 17th to 18th century. (Gewerbe-Museum, Bremen.)

8. Ornamental comb of dark tortoise-shell with gold lacquer decoration, wild goose and inlay of carved horn. Japan.

9. Ornamental comb in the form of a hovering peacock, wood with lacquer painting, green-tinted ivory and inlaid discs of mother of pearl. Japan.

10. Ornamental ivory comb with a two-colored gold lacquer branch and red coral berries. Japan. (Museum für Kunst and Gewerbe, Hamburg.)

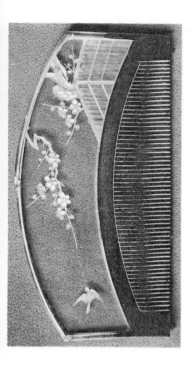
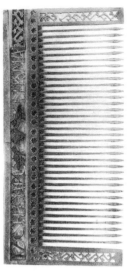

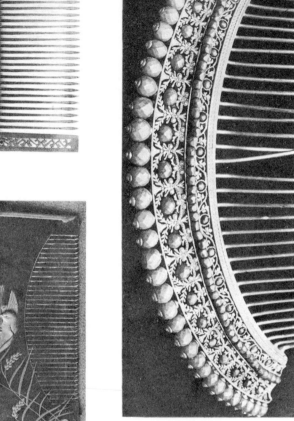
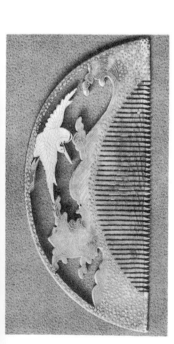
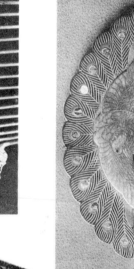
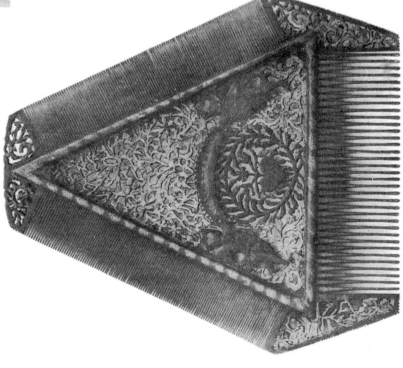

Plate 47

1. Ornamental piece (pendant) from a funerary mound in Pod-semel, Carniola.

2. Fibula from a funerary mound in Mosko, near Bilek, Herzego-vina.

3. Arm band with chain and pendants from a grave near Voghenza, province of Ferrara, Northern Italy.

4. Circular end of an iron object of the La Tène era in Central Europe (circa 400 B.C.). Place of discovery unknown.

5. Attachment from the burial grounds of Upper Koban in Ossetia, Caucasus.

6. Pendant (breast ornament) from the burial grounds on the Salz-berg near Hallstatt in Upper Austria.

7, 12. Pendant from the burial grounds of Santa Lucia on the Isonzo, (former) Küstenland, Austria.

8. Buckle ring from Hradischt near Strakonitz in Bohemia. Later La Tène era (1st century B.C.).

9. Pendant of hollow sheet metal (from a chain) from the Hall-statt burial grounds.

10, 22. Pendants from the Byčiskála cave near Brno, Moravia.

11. Pendant figure from a large belt ornament from Northern Italy.

13. Pendant from a funerary mound on the Glasinac in southeastern Bosnia.

14. Ornamental disc from the same place.

15. Pierced ornamental disc from a grave near Watsch in Carniola.

16, 23. Ornamental discs from a funerary mound on the Glasinac.

17. Pendant (breast ornament) from the Hallstatt burial grounds.

18, 20. Fibulas with free-hanging attachments from the burial grounds of Santa Lucia on the Isonzo.

19. Pendant from the Hallstatt burial grounds.

21. Ornamental ring of the La Tène era in Central Europe (circa 400 B.C.) from Hetzelsdorf, Gross-Kokel County, Transylvania.

24. Pendant from the same place.

25. Ornamental disc from the same place.

26. Ornamental disc from the Hallstatt burial grounds in Upper Austria.

27. Pendant from the burial grounds of Prazor near Otačac, Croatia.

28. Pendant in the form of a bulla with chains and beaver-tooth mount.

The originals of all the figures are of bronze.

With the exception of pieces 4, 8 and 21, all are from the so-called "early Iron Age" or "Hallstatt era" (circa 1000 to 400 B.C.).

(Naturhistorisches Museum, Vienna, Prehistoric Collection.)

Plate 48

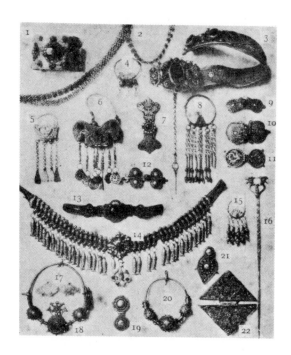

1, 13. Arm bands. Caucasus.

2. Chain. Caucasus.

3. Belt. Bokhara.

4–6, 8, 15, 18, 20. Earrings. Caucasus.

7, 9–12, 17, 19, 22. Clasps. Caucasus.

14. Necklace. Caucasus.

16. Hair pin. Caucasus.

21. Part of a clasp. Caucasus.

(Ethnographic Museum, Budapest.)

Figs. 5, 8, 13, 18, 20 described and illustrated in Count Zichy's *Travels,* Vol. I, Budapest, 1897.

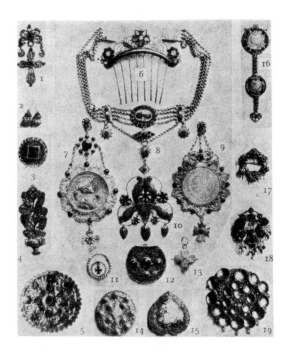

Plate 49

1. Pendant with cross from a peasant necklace, silver filigree work. 19th century. Bohemia.

2. Silver earring, filigree work. 19th century. Bohemia.

3. Metal piece from a man's belt, brass with carnelians. Tyrol.

4. Fragment of a Russian domestic altar. Raised and silvered copper.
(Náprstek Museum, Prague.)

5. Belt buckle, silver gilt with carnelians. Bulgaria.
(Ethnographic Division of the National Museum, Budapest.)

6. Comb, ornamental top set with stones. 19th century. Lusatia.

7. Pendant with commemorative medal, set with stones and pearls. 19th century. Bohemia.

8. Silver necklace with pendant. 19th century. Lusatia.

9. Pendant with commemorative medal. 19th century. Bohemia.

10. Ornament. 19th century. Westphalia.

11. Earring. 19th century. Lusatia.

12. Half of a clasp, silver filigree. Westphalia.

13. Silver pendant. Lusatia.
(Collection of the Verein für sächsische Volkskunde, Dresden.)

14. Buckle of silver filigree work. Sylt Island.

15. Amulet, silver filigree work with enamel painting. 19th century. France.

16. Silver necklace pendant, made from old gilded coins and Bohemian garnets. 19th century. Bohemia.

17. Man's shirt pin. 18th century. Norway.

18. Silver gilt brooch with black-oxidized pendants in the shape of crosses, modern workmanship. Norway.

19. Silver shirt pin. Norway.
(Náprstek Museum, Prague.)

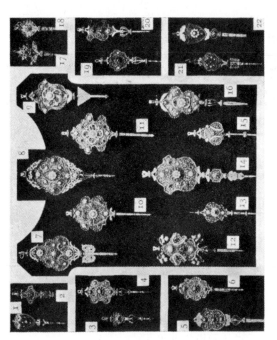

Plate 50

1–22. Silver filigree tags (bodice chain pendants). 19th century. Bavaria, Salzburg and Upper Austria. (Kunstgewerbe-Museum, Berlin.)

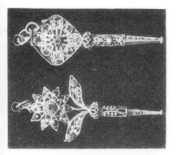
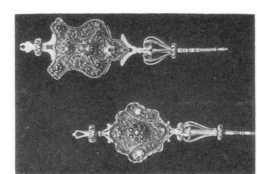
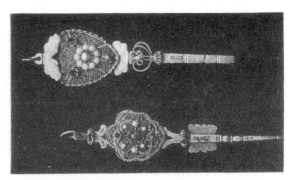
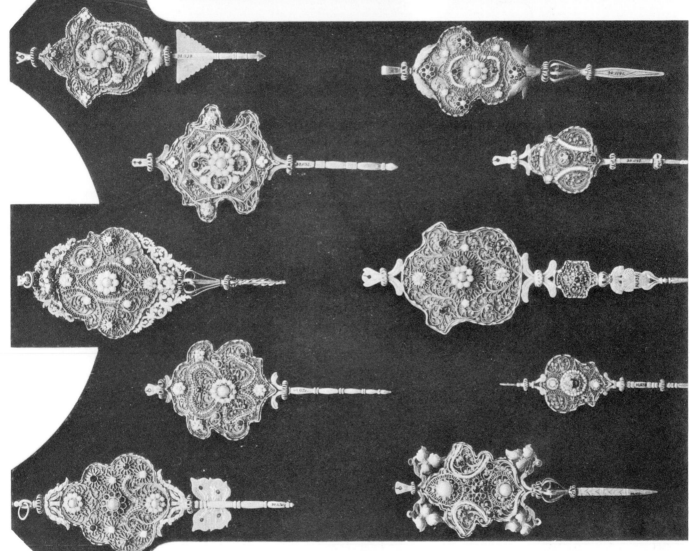

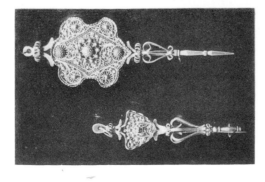

Plate 51

1. Silver necklace with enamel. India.
2. Gilded metal earrings. Jaypore, India.
3. Head ornament, braided work. Jodhpur, India.
4. Gilded metal arm band. Bombay, India.
5. Enameled silver arm band. India.
6, 8. Ornaments for the helix of the ear, gilded metal with pearls and stones. India.
7. Enameled silver toe ring. India.
9. Head ornament with green glass and pearls, gilded metal. India.
10. Gilded metal necklace. Bombay, India. (Österreichisches Museum für Kunst und Industrie, Vienna.)
11. Breast ornament. Switzerland. (Historisches Museum, Berne.)
12. Kalpak ornament, silver and enamel. Hungary.
13. Pair of earrings, silver gilt, with garnets and pearls, modern. Vienna, Austria.
14. Silver gilt earring. Balkan Peninsula. (Österreichisches Museum für Kunst und Industrie, Vienna.)

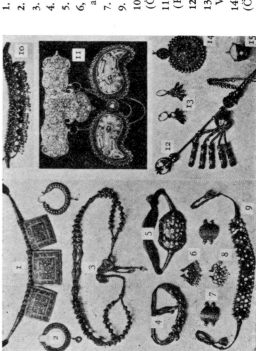

102

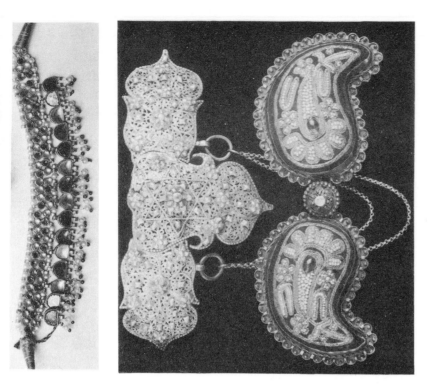

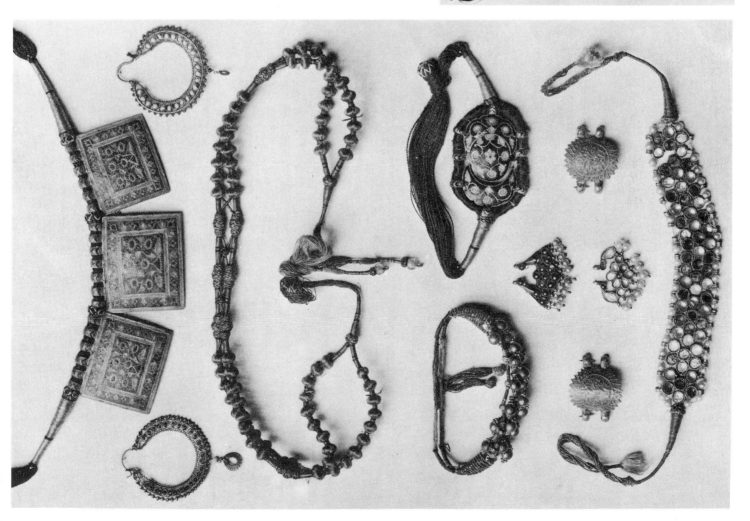

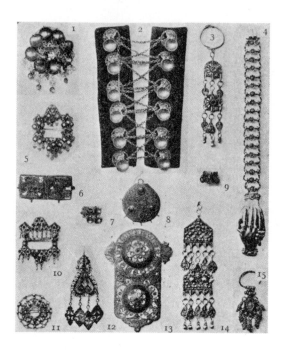

Plate 52

1. Shirt pin. 17th century. Norway.

2. Bodice trimming. 17th century. Norway.
(North Bohemian Commerce Museum, Reichenberg [Liberec], Bohemia.)

3. Silver nose ring. Syria.

4. Engagement arm band, gold. 19th century. Syria.
(Collection of Privy Councillor M. Rosenberg, Karlsruhe.)

5, 10. Six-cornered shirt buckles. 17th century. Norway.

6. Diptych with picture in relief. 17th century. Russia.

7. Broad ring with attached discs. 17th century. Norway.

8. Pendant adorned with filigree. 18th century. Russia.

9. Ring with movable circlets attached. Norway.

11. Wire-work pin. 17th century. Norway.
(North Bohemian Commerce Museum, Reichenberg [Liberec], Bohemia.)

12. Silver gilt peasant earring. 17th century. Russia.
(Collection of Privy Councillor M. Rosenberg, Karlsruhe.)

13. Part of a belt clasp with filigree and cloisonné enamel. 18th century. Russia.
(North Bohemian Commerce Museum, Reichenberg [Liberec], Bohemia.)

14. Earring. Syria.

15. Earring. 17th century. Russia.
(Collection of Privy Councillor M. Rosenberg, Karlsruhe.)

Plate 53

1–3, 5, 8, 10, 15, 17, 18. Rings with Egyptian symbols, gold. Ethiopia.

4, 16, 21. Gold earrings. Etruria.

6, 9, 13. Gold fibulas. Etruria.

7. Gold earring with pearls. Etruria.

11, 19, 20. Gold buttons. Etruria.

12. Amber rosette. Greece.

14. Gold ring with amethyst. Greece.

22. Gold arm band. Etruria.

(Neue Pinakothek, Munich.)

Plate 54

1. Amulet container. Turkestan.
2. Bronze ornament. Ob area. Siberia.
3, 6. Bronze ornaments. Caucasus.
4, 17. Breast and neck ornaments. Turkestan.
5. Earring. Kerch.
7. Part of a bronze clasp. Tiflis.
8. Earring. Caucasus.
9. Ornament from the central Ob area. Siberia.
10. Ear ornament of the Dungans. Turkestan.
11. Breast ornament for women. Turkestan.
12–16. Bronze ornaments. Central Ob area. Siberia.
(Ethnographic Division of the National Museum, Budapest.)

Plate 55

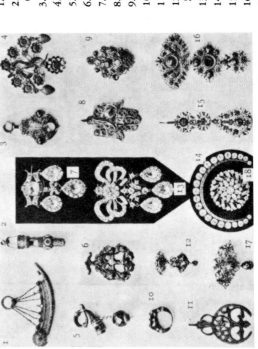

1. Silver and filigree hunting whistle. 18th century. Orient.
2. Ivory and silver hunting whistle. 16th to 17th century. Germany.
3. Gold pendant, Empire. Lower Germany.
4. Ornament of pietra dura and gilded copper. 17th century. Italy.
5. Hunting whistle of black horn with silver mount. 16th century.
6. Buckle with black stones. 17th century. Ulm.
7. Pendant with glass jewels. 17th to 18th century. Italy.
8. Silver amulet. 18th century. Cairo.
9. Pendant of silver gilt with enamel. 17th century. Italy.
10. Gold ring with precious stones. Late Imperial period. Roman.
11. Silver amulet, modern. Egypt.
12. Pendant (for the "3," see Plate 31, No. 9). Around 1600. Southern Germany.
13. Pendant with glass jewels. 17th century. Italy.
14. Half-moon with glass jewels and blue enamel. 18th century.
15. Earring with stones, gold and silver. 18th century. Brabant.
16. Pendant with roses. 17th to 18th century. Brabant.
17. Gold ornament. 18th to 19th century. Brabant.
18. Button with glass jewels. 18th century.
(Collection of Privy Councillor M. Rosenberg, Karlsruhe.)

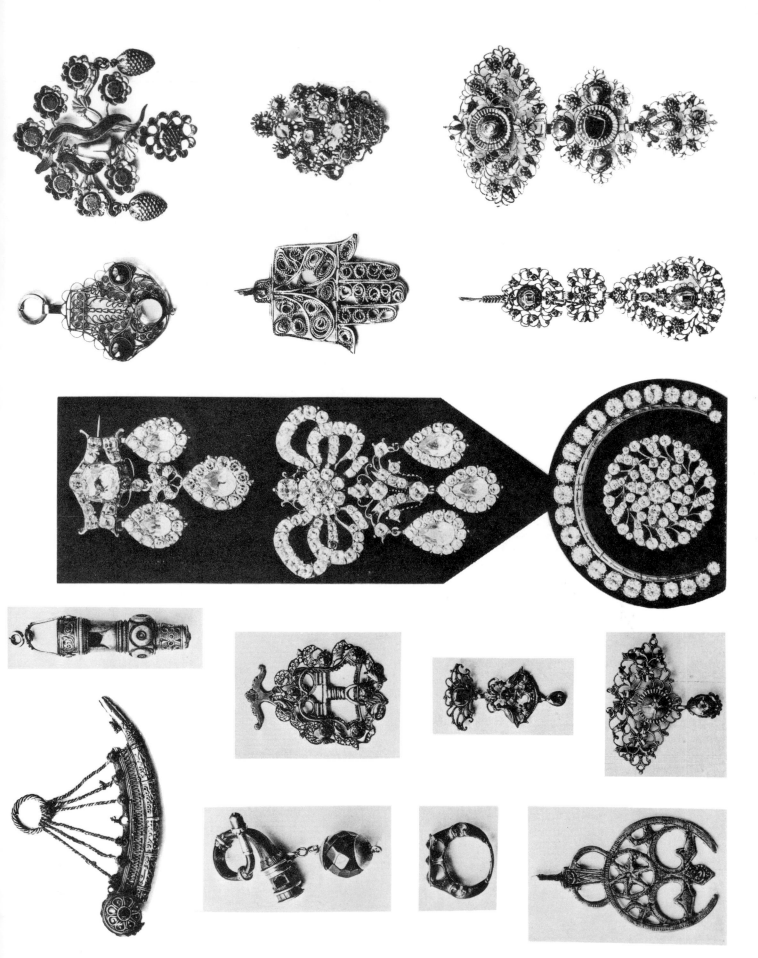

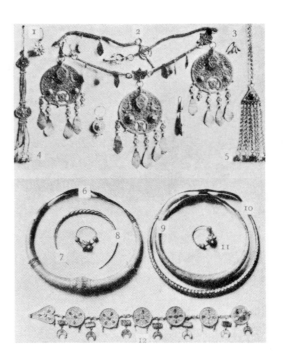

Plate 56

1, 3. Ear ornaments of yellow metal. Bulgaria.

2. Breast ornament of silver filigree. Bulgaria (Zagora).

4. Watch chain of silver wire, old workmanship. Bulgaria (Varna).

5. Watch chain with gilded clasps. Montenegro.
(Naturhistorisches Museum, Vienna, Ethnographic Collection.)

6. Silver waist band, partially gilded. Galicia. (Austria)

7. Silver neck ring. Galicia.

8. Silver earring. Galicia.

9, 10. Silver waist bands. Galicia.

11. Silver earring. Galicia.

12. Silver horse chain with filigree work and beads from the time of the Turkish wars. Found in Galicia, 1846. Galicia.
(Kunsthistorisches Museum, Vienna.)

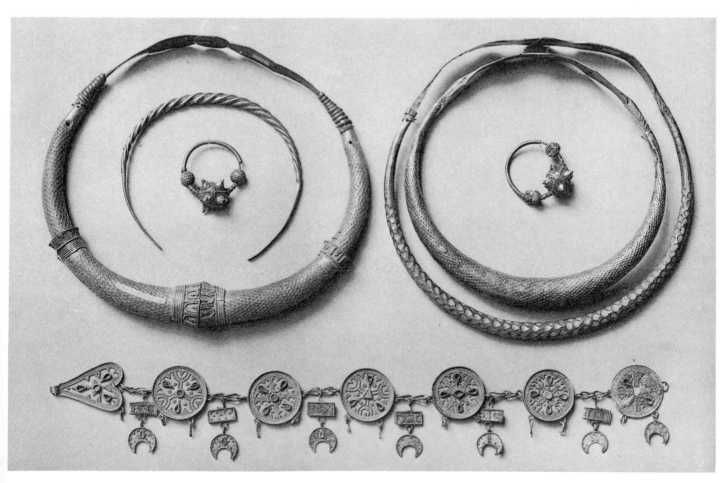

Plate 57

1, 6. Breast pendants. Switzerland (Graubünden).

2. Necklace pendant. Switzerland (Zurich).

3. Necklace, enameled gold. Switzerland (Zurich).

4, 16. Gold earrings. Switzerland (Engadin).

5. Cuff links. Switzerland (Nidwalden).

7. Pendant with the arms of Nägeli-Bern (made of an apricot pit). Switzerland (Berne).

8. Earring. Switzerland (Chur).

9. Chain Link. Switzerland.

10. Necklace, so-called *Blättlikette* (little leaf chain). Switzerland. Canton Appenzeller.

11. Enameled gold necklace. Switzerland (Zurich).

12. Enameled gold breast pendant. Switzerland (Zurich).

13. Ring. Switzerland (Canton Solothurn).

14. Necklace. Gold filigree with coral beads. Switzerland (Canton Schwyz).

15. Gold ring. Switzerland (Engadin).

17. Cross, rock crystal with gold, enamel and stones. Switzerland (Canton Aargau).

(Landes-Museum, Zurich.)

Plate 58

1. Gold buckle. Hungary.

2. Gold ring. Period of the migrations (Völkerwanderung). Hungary.

3, 6, 17, 19, 20, 23. Gold earrings. Hungary.

4. Gold fibula with rock crystal, carnelians and sardonyx. Szilágysomló, Transylvania.

5. Cicada fibula, gold with garnets. Sáranberke, Hungary.

7. Gold pendant, formerly adorned with stones. Hungary.

8. Gold arm band with garnets. Puszta-Bakod, Hungary.

9. Gold arm band. Hungary.

10. Gold plate representing an animal. Hungary.

11. Gold hair pin with garnets. Hungary.

12. Gold arm band. Hungary.

13. Gold fibula. Hungary.

14. Gold ring. Hungary.

15. Gold earring with garnets. Hungary.

16. Silver earring with silver-plate beads. Csiko, Hungary.

18. Gold pendant with garnet inlays, from the Apahida find. Hungary.

21. Gold arm band with garnets. Szilágysomló, Transylvania.

22. Gold fibula with rock crystal and enameling. Szilágysomló, Transylvania.

(National Museum, Budapest.)

Plate 59

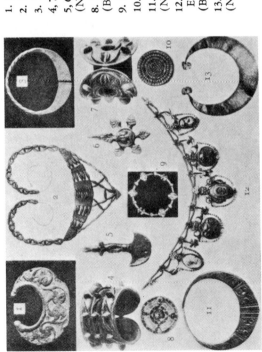

1. Half-moon. Bronze armor ornament. Anglo-Saxon.
2. Necklace of jet beads with plating. Anglo-Saxon.
3. Brooch of massive silver. Anglo-Saxon.
4, 7. Bronze arm bands. Anglo-Saxon.
5, 6. Parts of ornaments. Anglo-Saxon.
(National Museum, Edinburgh.)
8. Brooch with enamel. Anglo-Saxon.
(British Museum, London.)
9. Silver ornament. Anglo-Saxon.
10. Bronze brooch with enamel. Anglo-Saxon.
11. Bronze neck band. Anglo-Saxon.
(National Museum, Edinburgh.)
12. Necklace, gold with enamel and ancient cameos. 19th century. England.
(British Museum, London.)
13. Half-moon, engraved metal. Anglo-Saxon.
(National Museum, Edinburgh.)

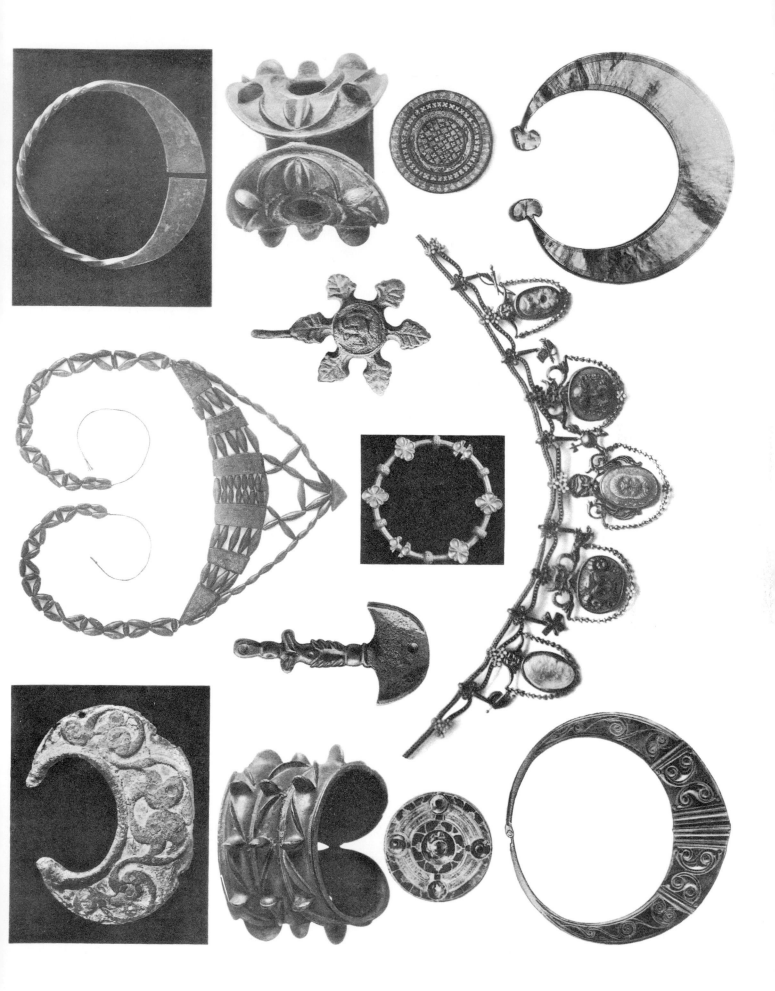

Plate 60

1–4, 7–10. Pubic coverings. Java.

5. Amulet (part of a tiger bone in a silver mount). Java.

6. Arm band. Java.

11. Ear ornament. Timor (Sunda Islands).

12. Necklace. Balkan Peninsula.
(Ethnographic Division of the National Museum, Budapest.)

13–16. Crosses to be worn hanging from the neck. Galicia.

17. Copper pipe reamer. Bojken, Galicia.

18, 20, 22. Brass crosses worn on the neck. Bojken, Galicia.

19, 21. Brass clasps. Bojken, Galicia.

23. Necklace of the Bojken, glass and brass beads. Galicia.
(Museum für Österreichische Volkskunde, Vienna.)

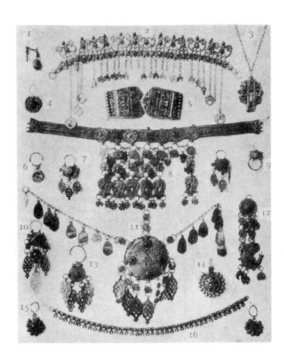

Plate 61

1. Silver earring.
2. Forehead ornament, brass.
3. Cross with chain, plated German silver.
4. Earring, plated German silver with red stone.
5. Brass belt clasp with mosaic.
6, 7, 10, 13, 14. Earrings, plated German silver.
8. Brass necklace.
9. Brass ring.
11. Plated German silver necklace.
12. Brass hair pendant with mosaic.
15. Earring, plated German silver with red stone.
16. Necklace, gilded brass.
(Czechoslovakian Ethnographic Museum, Prague.)
All the objects on this plate are Bosnian women's jewelry.

Plate 62

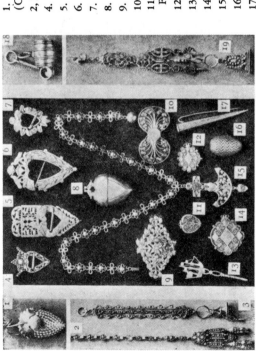

1. Silver pendant for a peasant chain. Bavaria. (Collection of A. Merklein, goldsmith, Nuremberg.)
2, 3. Steel chains. England (Birmingham).
4. Silver blouse pin. East Frisia (Goltland).
5. Silver buckle for shepherd's smock. Württemberg (Laupheim).
6. Silver blouse buckle. East Frisia (Strackholt).
7. Silver blouse buckle. East Frisia (Nortmoor).
8. Silver snuff box, heart-shaped, with doves. East Frisia (Leer).
9. Silver buckle for man's hat. Württemberg (Biberach).
10. Silver gilt belt buckle. East Frisia (Ihrhove).
11. Heart-shaped silver snuff box with four compartments. East Frisia (Loga).
12. Silver crown clasp. East Frisia (Leer).
13. Silver pipe reamer. East Frisia (Leer).
14. Silver crown clasp. East Frisia (Gesel).
15. Silver chain with anchor-shaped pendant. Oldenburg (Jever).
16. Silver snuff box (egg-shaped). East Frisia (Aurich).
17. Silver case for knitting needles. East Frisia (Weener). (Collection of C. Esslinger, Postal Director, Leer, East Frisia.)
18. Silver pendant for a peasant chain. Bavaria. (Collection of A. Mecklein, goldsmith, Nuremberg.)
19. Steel chain. England (Birmingham).

Plate 63

1, 12, 13. Earring. Northern India.

2. Nose ring. India.

3, 6, 9, 10. Toe ring. Southern India.

4, 14. Earrings. Northern India (Peshawar).

5. Earring. India.

7. Foot band. Southern India.

8. Arm band. Northern India.

11. Amulet. Northern India.

15. Amulet. Northern India.

16. Necklace. India.

(Naturhistorisches Museum, Vienna, Ethnographic Collection.)

Plate 64

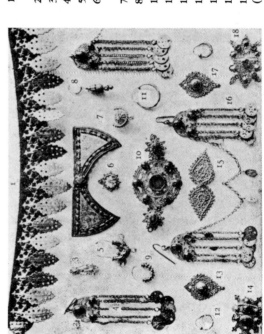

1. Bridal ornament, forehead band, gilded metal pieces on velvet. 18th century. Egerland.
2. Hair ornament, silver gilt set with stones. Dalmatia.
3. Gold earring. Herzegovina.
4. Belt clasp. Herzegovina.
5. Gold earring. Istria.
6. Pendant, copper and enamel picture in a gold frame. Herzegovina.
7, 9. Gold earrings. Istria.
8. Earring, pearls mounted in gold. Herzegovina.
10. Clasp, silver gilt set with stones. Dalmatia.
11, 12. Gold earrings. Istria.
13. Part of a bridal ornament, silver gilt. Dalmatia.
14. Clasp, silver gilt set with stones. Dalmatia.
15, 17. Part of a breast ornament, silver gilt. Dalmatia.
16. Hair pendant, silver gilt set with stones. Dalmatia.
18. Clasp, silver gilt set with stones. Dalmatia.
(Museum für Österreichische Volkskunde, Vienna.)

128

Plate 65

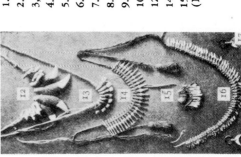

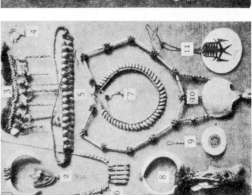

1. Nose ornament. New Guinea.
2. Neck ornament. Solomon Islands.
3, 11. Breast ornament. New Guinea.
4. Neck ornament. Solomon Islands.
5. Women's forehead band. Samoa.
6. Necklace. Marshall Islands.
7. Forehead ornament. New Guinea.
8. Arm ornament. New Guinea.
9. Breast ornament. Solomon Islands.
10. Neck and breast ornament. Tonga Islands.
12, 13. Breast ornament. Borneo.
14. Neck ornament. Vancouver (North America).
15–17. Neck and ear ornaments. Brazil.
(Naturhistorisches Museum, Vienna, Ethnographic Collection.)

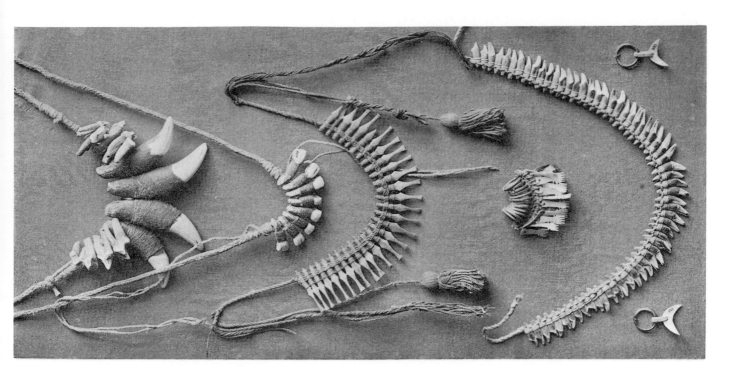

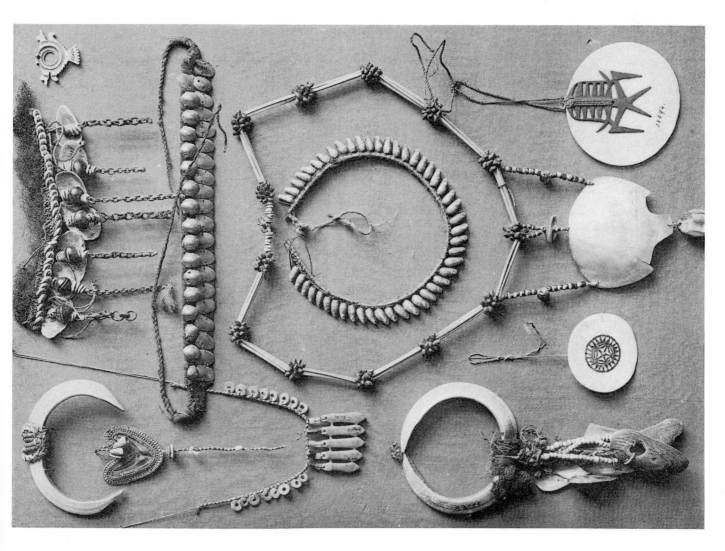

Plate 66

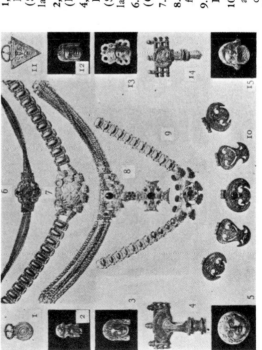

1, 11. Buckles, gold plate, late Roman. Found in Sacrau near Breslau.
(Schlesisches Museum für Kunstgewerbe und Altertümer, Breslau.)

2, 3, 5, 12. Bronze masks.
(Kunsthistorisches Museum, Vienna.)

4, 14. Crossbow fibulas of silver decorated with gold, late Roman. Found in Sacrau near Breslau.
(Schlesisches Museum für Kunstgewerbe und Altertümer, Breslau.)

6. Silver folk ornament. Lusatia.
(Collection of Tillmann-Schmitt, Breslau.)

7. Silver plate chain, first half of 19th century. Silesia (Gebirge).

8. Silver folk ornament with red garnets and green glass jewels, first half of 19th century. Silesia.

9. Silver folk ornament with red stone, first half of 19th century. Lower Silesia (Gebirge region).

10. Five parts of a gold-plate breast ornament with rich filigree and granulated decoration, on the center piece a reddish brown carnelian. Late Roman. Found in Sacrau near Breslau.
(Schlesisches Museum für Kunstgewerbe und Altertümer, Breslau.)

13. Mask of Athena, trimming of a bucket.

15. Mask of a river god.
(Kunsthistorisches Museum, Vienna.)

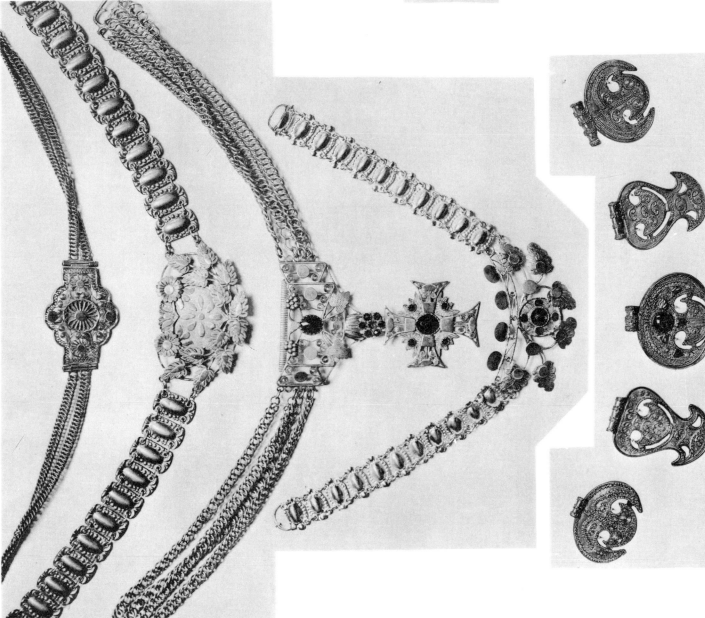

Plate 67

1. Clasp for an apron, silver. Northern Holland.

2. Shoe buckle, silver fastened to leather.

3. Head covering, clasp, which encloses the whole back of a woman's head, gold. Frisia.

4. Silver gilt clasp on which sewing utensils can be hung. Northern Holland.

5. Buckle for an apron, filigree work in silver or goid. Northern Holland.

7. Silver gilt clasp (for gathering up dresses). Northern Holland.

8. Breast chain, silver gilt, fastened at the shoulders. Northern Holland.

9. Diamond buckle for a chain of pearls, coral or garnets.

10. Silver watch chain. Netherlands.

11. Head covering (iron, silver or gold); the two rings below are to be buckled into diamond ear buttons. Southern Holland.

12. Clasp of a garment, silver gilt. Northern Holland.

13. Head covering of red burnished gold, adorned with diamonds and gold rosettes.

14. Belt buckle, silver gilt. Northern Holland.

15. Gold buckle for pearl or coral necklace. Northern Holland.

16. "Heart" (fastening) of a work bag. Northern Holland.

17. Silver buckle for long stockings. Northern Holland.
(Collection of E. Voetz, Haarlem, Holland.)
[NOTE: There is no number 6.]

Plate 68

1. Comb. Lower German.

2. Comb. Spain.

3. Comb. Southern Germany.

4, 5. Combs. Lower German.
(North Bohemian Commerce Museum, Reichenberg [Liberec], Bohemia.)

6. Pendant, filigree work. Switzerland.

7. Ladies' comb.

8. Necklace of thin punched silver gilt leaves. Switzerland.

9. Woman's belt of twisted wires in filigree work, brass with imitation jewels. Switzerland.

10. Silver brooch with tassels in filigree work. Switzerland.

11. Silver stickpins in filigree work. Switzerland.

12. Silver buckle in filigree work (so-called *Knüpferli*). Switzerland.

13. Arm band with clasp, filigree work. Switzerland.

14. Pendant in filigree work. Switzerland.

15. Rosary with garnet beads, filigree balls and a pilgrimage coin. Switzerland.

(Landes-Museum, Zurich.)

Plate 69

1, 4. Gilded copper necklaces. 19th century. India.

2, 5. Silver ankle rings. 19th century. Turkey.

3. Gilded brass arm band. 19th century. India.

6. Necklace. 1870–1880. Brass on a brightly colored silk cord. India (Bombay).

7. Hair ornament. 19th century. Brass. India.

8. Necklace. 1870–1880. Gold. India.
(Kunstgewerbe-Museum, Berlin.)

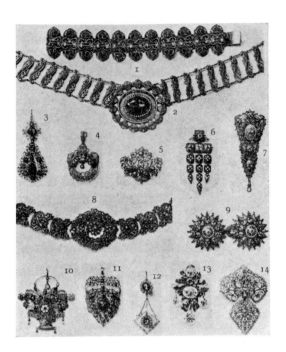

Plate 70

1. Arm band, filigree, silver gilt, modern work.
2. Gold necklace, Empire, around 1820. Austria.
3. Pear-shaped earring, silver gilt. 18th to 19th century. France.
4. Earring, filigree.
5. Silver gilt brooch. 18th century. Spain.
6. Pendant with blue and white enameled fields. 19th century. France.
7. Silver gilt chatelaine. 19th century. France.
8. Gold filigree arm band. 18th century. Frisia.
9. Two-part brooch. 19th century. France.
10. Silver filigree pendant. 18th century. Tyrol.
11. Pierced silver pendant. France.
12. Gold and enamel earring, Empire. France.
13. Silver brooch, partially gilded, with pear-shaped white enamel attachments, circa 1760. Germany.
14. Gold pendant. 18th century. Normandy.

(North Bohemian Commerce Museum, Reichenberg [Liberec], Bohemia.)

Plate 71

1, 12, 35. Pins from the burial grounds of Upper Koban, about 1000 B.C. Caucasus.

2. Fibula, period of migrations. Central Europe.

3, 28. Earrings from the burial grounds of Keszthely, silver filigree with vitreous paste. Period of migrations. Hungary.

4, 5, 29, 42. Animal fibulas, late Roman.

6. Ornamental ring, silver. Period of migrations. Marchegg, Lower Austria.

7, 8, 9, 11, 22, 23, 36. Pins from the lake dwellings of Peschione on Lake Garda. 2000 B.C. Italy.

10. Final link of a heavy chain, enameled bronze. 1000 B.C. Bohemia.

13. Roman ornament from the ruins of Brigetio, Hungary.

14. Pin with protector, about 1000 B.C. Hallstatt, Upper Austria.

15. Fibula, early Imperial period. Sissek, Croatia.

16. Roman animal fibula. Brigetio, Hungary.

17. Part of a buckle, period of migrations. Keszthely, Hungary.

18. Earring, Middle Ages. Moscow region.

19, 24. Ornamental trims, Roman. Brigetio, Hungary.

20. Late Roman fibula.

21, 30, 33, 44, 45. Roman ornamental pieces. Brigetio, Hungary.

25, 26. Pins, about 1000 B.C. Hallstatt, Upper Austria.

27. Human figures, about 100 B.C. Near Strakonitz, Bohemia.

31. Roman fibula. Central Europe.

32. Roman buckle ring. Brigetio, Hungary.

34. Ornamental disc from Deutsch-Krottingen, Middle Ages.

37. Roman buckle. Brigetio, Hungary.

38. Belt catch, 100 B.C. Strakonitz, Bohemia.

39. Etruscan belt catch. Italy.

40. Belt catch, period of migrations. Central Europe.

41. Fibula. Roman Imperial period.

43. Animal figure, about 100 B.C. Central Europe.
All bronze, unless otherwise specified.
(National Museum, Budapest.)

142

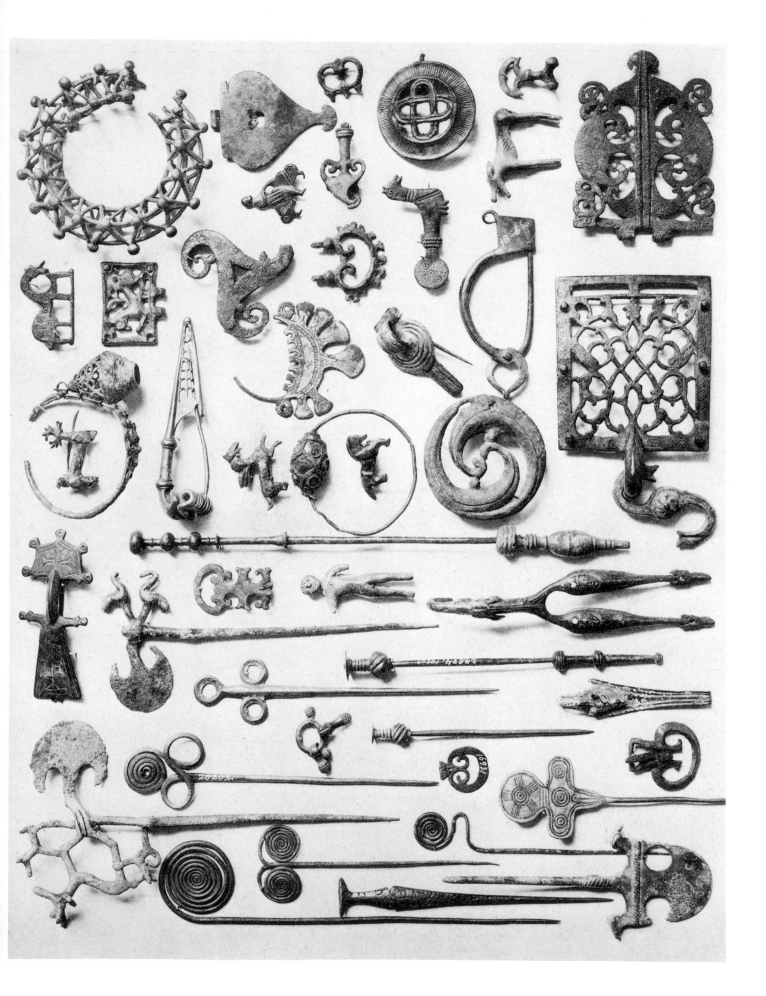

Plate 72

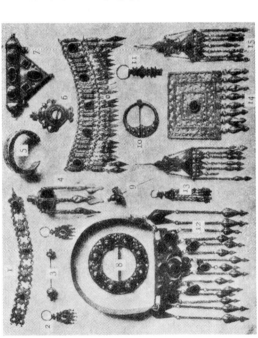

1. Ornamental chain. Tekke-Turkmenian. Russia (Transcaspian region).
2, 11, 13. Earrings. Turkestan.
3. Ornament. Turkestan.
4, 7. Ornaments. Tekke-Turkmenian. Russia (Transcaspian region).
5. Arm clasp. Tekke-Turkmenian. Russia (Transcaspian region).
6. Brooch. Turkestan.
8. Brooch. Russia (Transcaspian region).
9. Pin. Caucasus.
10. Brooch, modern workmanship.
12. Neck and breast ornament. Tekke-Turkmenian.
14. Part of an ornamental pendant. Tekke-Turkmenian.
15. Earring. Tekke-Turkmenian.
(Museum für Völkerkunde, Leipzig.)

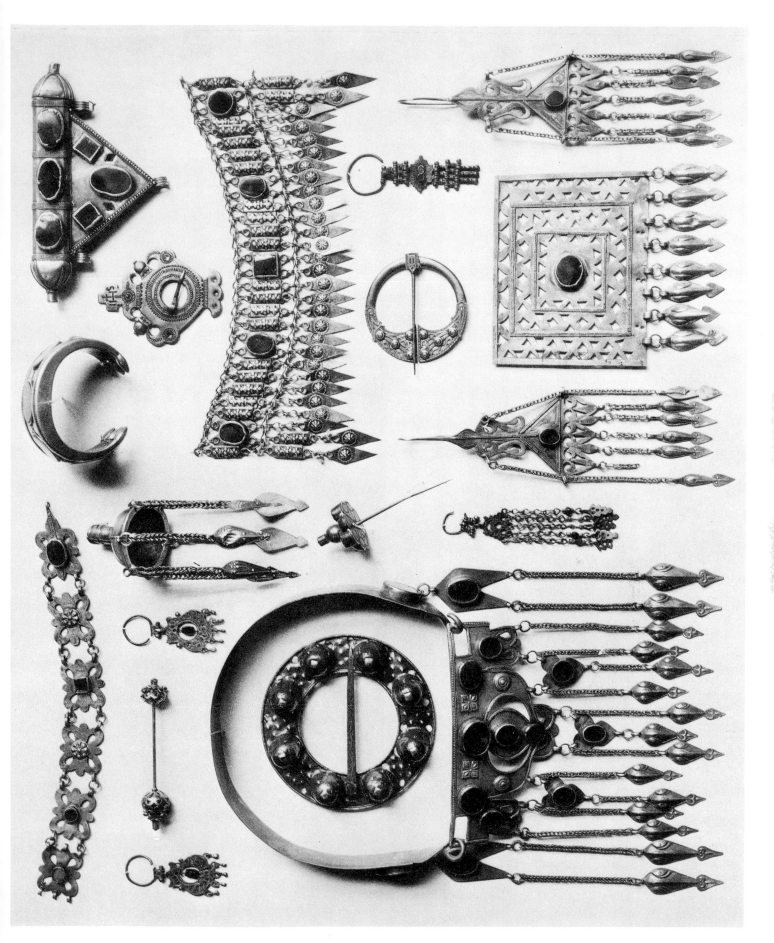

Plate 73

1, 3, 5. Arm bands. India.

2. Neck and breast ornament. India.

4. Earring. Northern India.

6. Arm band. Kashmir.

7, 11. Amulets. Southern India.

8, 12. Foot bands. Southern India.

9, 13. Arm bands. Southern India.

10. Rattling foot band. Southern India.

(Naturhistorisches Museum, Ethnographic Collection, Vienna.)

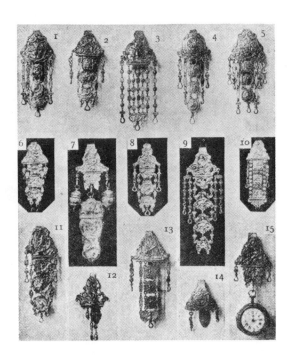

Plate 74

1–5, 11–15. Chatelaines. Silver gilt. Germany.
(National Museum, Budapest.)

6. Chatelaine. Gilded bronze. Mid-18th century. Germany.

7. Chatelaine with three pendants in the shape of covered boxes.
Gilded and partially painted in cold lacquer colors. Germany.

8. Chatelaine, bronze. Mid-18th century. Germany.

9. Silver gilt chatelaine. Germany.

10. Gilded bronze chatelaine. Germany.
(Kunstgewerbe-Museum, Berlin.)

Plate 75

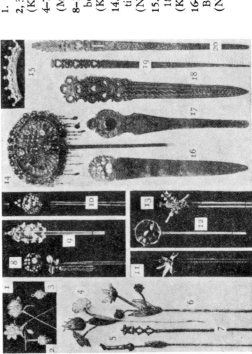

1. Hair pins. 19th century. Malta.
2, 3. Filigree buttons. 18th to 19th century. Greece. (Kunstgewerbe-Museum, Berlin.)
4–7. Silver filigree hair pins. Tyrol (Ampezzo). (Museum für Österreichische Volkskunde, Vienna.)
8–13. Silver hair pins, partially gilded and adorned with coral beads. End of the 19th century. Japan. (Kunstgewerbe-Museum, Berlin.)
14. Iron hair pin, the head decorated with a mirror and with silver tinsel imitation garnets. 18th century. Stechoric near Prague. (Náprstek Museum, Prague.)
15. Top of a comb, gold plate, filigree and pearls. End of the 18th century. Venice. (Kunstgewerbe-Museum, Berlin.)
16–20. Brass hair pins, part of the Leitomischl traditional costume. Budislav near Leitomischl in Bohemia. (Náprstek Museum, Prague.)

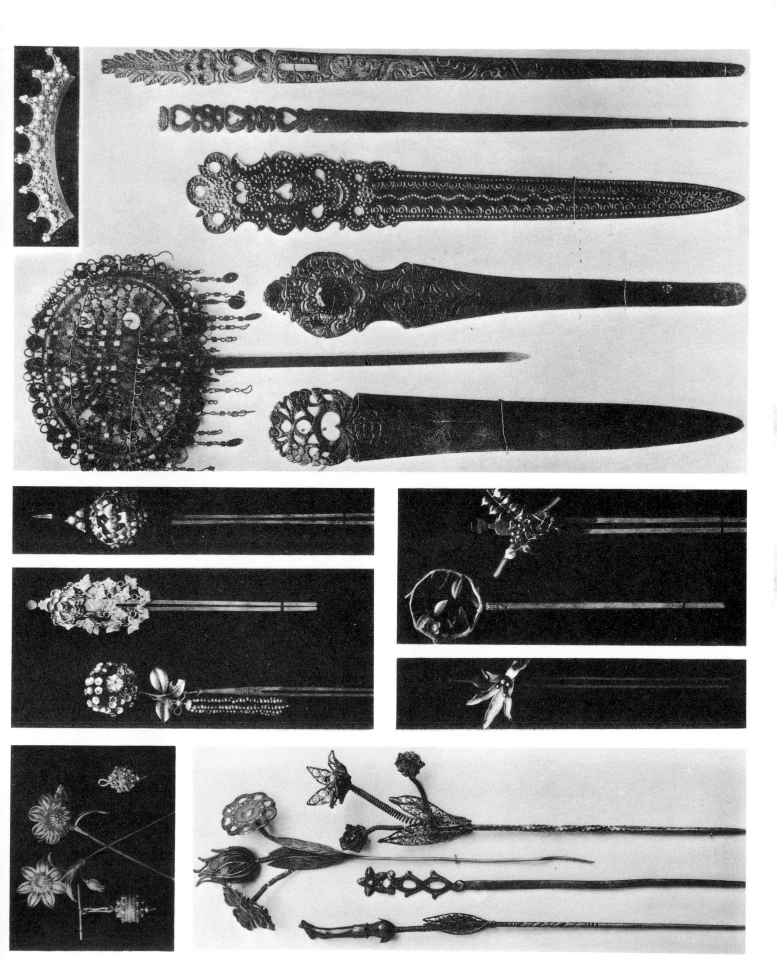

Plate 76

1, 3, 11, 14. Pocket watches, about 1600. Germany.

2. Ladies' belt, silver. Germany.

4. Earring of wax pearls. Germany.

6, 8, 9, 10. Silver filigree buckles, gilded. 18th to 19th century. Norway.
(Kunstgewerbe-Museum, Berlin.)

7. Necklace of wax pearls. Germany.

7A. Necklace of wax pearls. Germany.

12. Brooch with 7 small medals bearing the attributes of the 7 Ionic Islands, circa 1873. Greece.

13. Brooch. 19th century. Malta.
(Kunstgewerbe-Museum, Dresden.)
[NOTE: Number 5 is not described.]

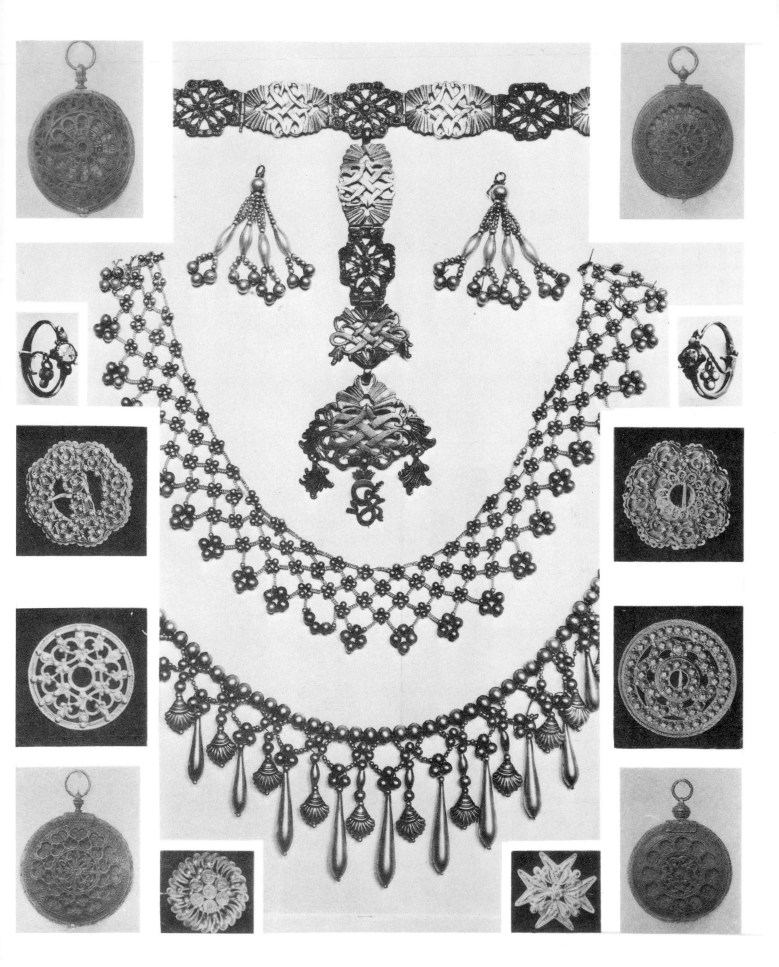

Plate 77

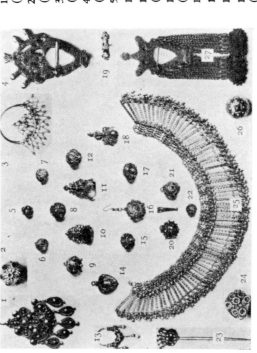

1. Brass earring. Hungary.
(Náprstek Museum, Prague.)
2. Button set with stones. Bavaria (Alpine area).
(Kunstgewerbe-Museum, Nuremberg.)
3. Silver earring. Dzungaria (Central Asia).
(Ethnographic Division of the National Museum, Budapest.)
4. Blouse clasp (*spinka*). Hungarian Slovakia.
(Náprstek Museum, Prague.)
5–9. Buttons. 18th century. Southern Germany.
10, 11. Signets. Beginning of the 18th century. Southern Germany.
12, 20, 21, 22. Buttons. 17th century. Southern Germany.
(Kunstgewerbe-Museum, Dresden.)
13. Earring. 16th to 17th century. Origin unknown.
(Kunstgewerbe-Museum, Nuremberg.)
14. Gilded bronze pendant. 17th century. Germany.
15, 17. Buttons. 18th century. Frisia.
16. Tag for a cord. 19th century. Bavaria.
18. Pendant, signet. 17th century. Germany.
(Kunstgewerbe-Museum, Dresden.)
19. Golden engagement ring, made of two circlets that can be put together. Germany.
(Kunstgewerbe-Museum, Nuremberg.)
23. Silver gilt breast pin. Bokhara, Turkestan.
(Ethnographic Division of the National Museum, Budapest.)
24. Ring. Sweden.
(Kunstgewerbe-Museum, Nuremberg.)
25. Silver necklace. India.
(Kunstgewerbe-Museum, Dresden.)
26. Button. Bavaria (Alpine region).
(Kunstgewerbe-Museum, Nuremberg.)
27. Blouse clasp from Marikorá, Hungarian Slovakia.
(Náprstek Museum, Prague.)

154

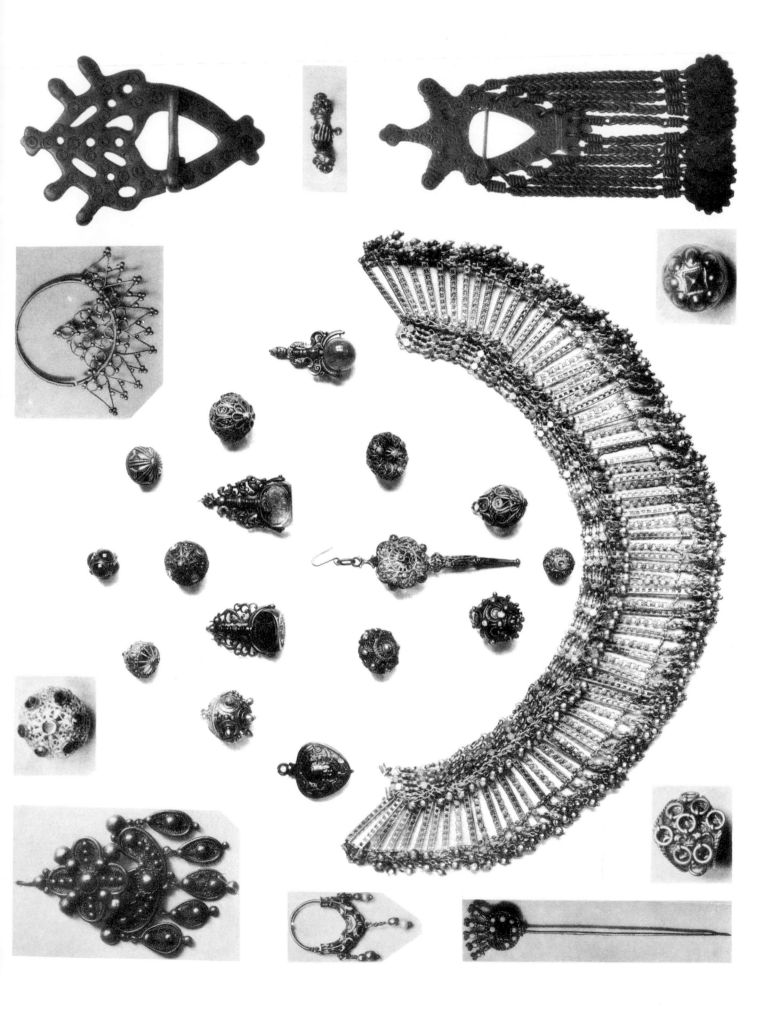

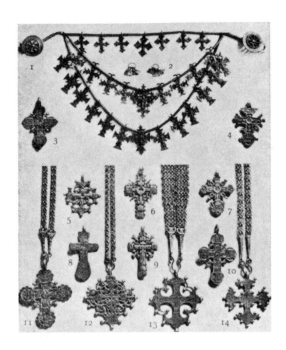

Plate 78

1. Brass necklace, Huzul workmanship from the Carpathians. 19th century. East Galicia.

2. Brass-plate earrings, Bojken workmanship from the Carpathians. 19th century. East Galicia.
(Náprstek Museum, Prague.)

3–14. Pendant crosses for Russian Orthodox priests. Russia.
(Königliche Zeichen-Akademie, Hanau.)

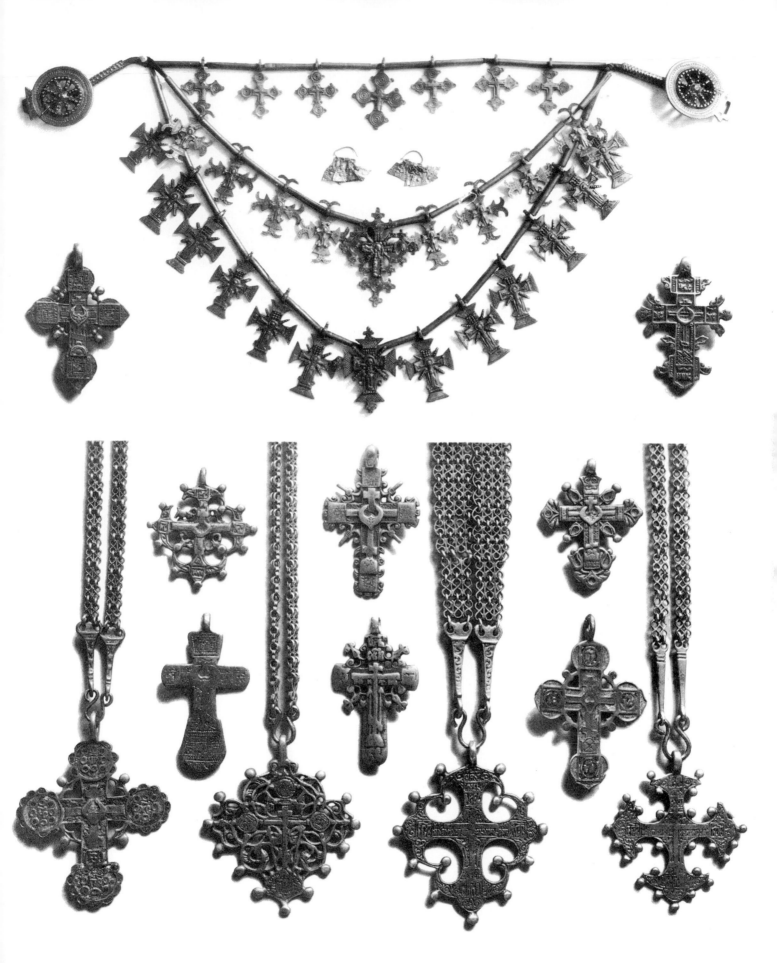

Plate 79

1–3, 5, 7–11, 13, 14, 16, 17, 20, 23, 24, 26, 27, 29, 30. Parts of ornaments, mostly brass, damascened. Persia.

4. Earring. Persia.

6, 12, 18. Neck ornaments, silver with enamel and damascening. India.

15. Pendant, tiger claws with gold filigree. India.

19. Brooch. Persia.

21. Brass pendant. Persia.

22. Ornamental disc of a toe ring, brass. India.

25. Brass clasp. Persia.

28. Middle piece of an ornament, brass. Persia.

(Museum für Völkerkunde, Leipzig.)

Plate 80

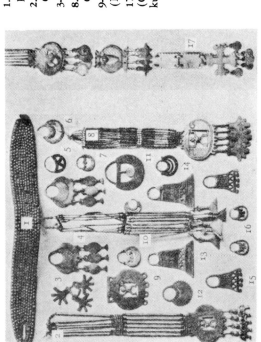

1. Neck ornament of the Araucanians, leather with silver plates and pearls. Chile.
2. Pendant of the Araucanians, silver lamina and silver beads. Chile.
3–7. Ear jewelry of the Araucanians, silver. Chile.
8. Pendant of the Araucanians, silver platelets with chains of seeds. Chile.
9–16. Ear jewelry of the Araucanians. Chile. (Naturhistorisches Museum, Ethnographic Collection, **Vienna.**)
17. Pendant of the Araucanians, silver. Chile. (Grossherzoglich Badische Sammlung für Altertümer und **Völker-kunde, Karlsruhe.**)

160

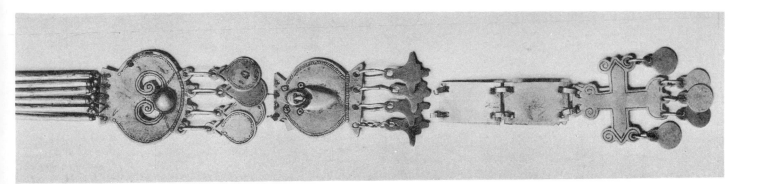

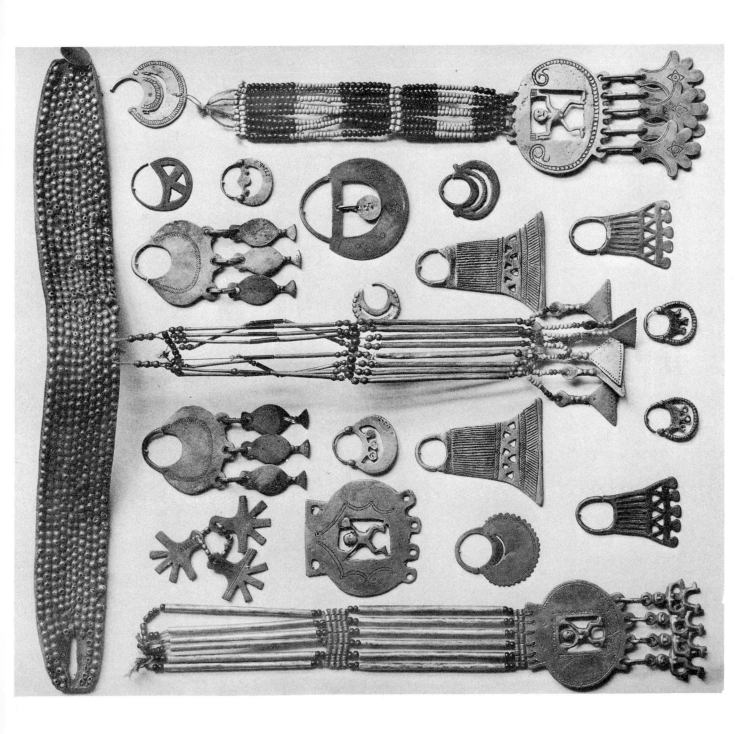

Plate 81

1. Pin (found in Pritzwalk), silver. 14th century. Brandenburg Marches.

2. Part of a breast pendant, partially gilded and set with stones. 18th to 19th century. Greece.

3. Buckle. 18th century. Norway.
(Kunstgewerbe-Museum, Berlin.)

4. Peasant woman's fibula. Finland.
(Ethnographic Division of the National Museum, Budapest.)

5. Silver filigree brooch. South Tyrol.
(North Bohemian Commerce Museum, Reichenberg [Liberec], Bohemia.)

6. Gilded brass necklace. Westphalia.

7, 8. Gilded silver pendants with commemorative medals. Bohemia.

9. Silver earring. Lusatia.

10. Part of a clasp, silver. Lusatia.

11. Silver necklace. Lusatia.

12, 17, 18. Rings. Lusatia.

13. Gilded silver pendant. Lusatia.

14, 16. Parts of clasps, gold and silver, filigree. Lusatia.
(Collection of the Verein für Sächsische Volkskunde, Dresden.)

15. Necklace. Southern Germany.

19. Silver gilt neck pendant. Northern Germany.

20. Silver gilt earring. Northern Germany.
(Collection of Theodor Heiden, court jeweler, Munich.)

Plate 82

1, 4, 6, 9, 11–17. Hair combs. (Former) German New Guinea.

2, 3, 5, 7. Hair combs. Samoa.

8, 10. Hair combs. Somali.

18, 19. Hair combs. Admiralty Islands.
(Ethnographic Division of the National Museum, Budapest.)

20. Arm band. Benin, Africa.

21. Arm band of the Masai. Africa.

22. Arm bands. Cameroon.

23–25. Arm bands. Benin, Africa.

26–32. Arm bands. New Guinea and Solomon Islands.
(Naturhistorisches Museum, Vienna, Ethnographic Collection.)

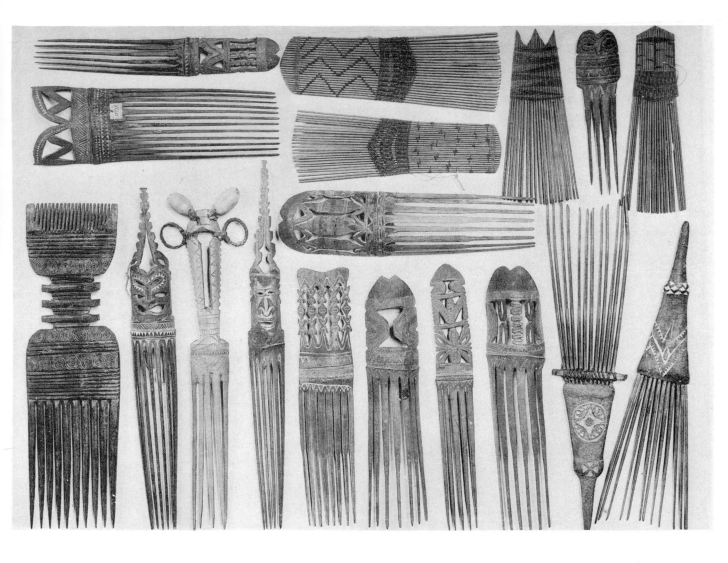

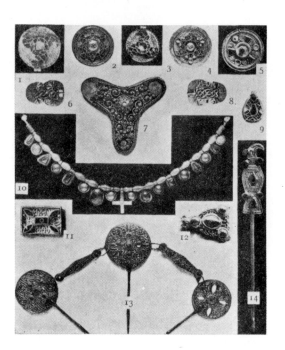

Plate 83

1–5, 9. Anglo-Saxon gold ornaments. 6th century. England.

6, 8. Anglo-Saxon gold buckles. 7th century. England.

7. Silver ornament. 9th century. Scandinavia.

10. Anglo-Saxon gold necklace with garnets. 7th century. England.

11. Anglo-Saxon gold ornament with garnets. 6th century. England.

12. Bronze pendant. England.

13. Gilded bronze pin. 9th century. England.

14. Anglo-Saxon pin. Metal unknown. 6th century. England.
(British Museum, London. [P. G. Konody.])

Plate 84

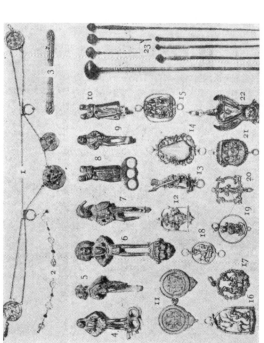

1. Roman necklace (from the gold hoard in Nieder-Lunnern). Switzerland.
2. Roman arm band. Gold. Switzerland.
3. Roman arm band. Massive gold plate. Switzerland. (Landes-Museum, Zurich.)
4–10. Key ring hooks from Brienz. (Costume of the 15th century.) Nuremberg.
11. Parts of ornaments with the Virgin and Child and the Resurrection. Byzantine.
12. Pendant with the Virgin surrounded by angels. 15th century.
13. Pendant of the Order of St. George. 16th century.
14. Pendant with chalcedony.
15. Pendant with the Coronation of the Virgin. 15th century.
16. St. Hubert pendant. 16th century.
17. Pendant with St. Anne, the Virgin and Child. 15th century.
18. Pendant with St. George. 15th century.
19. Pendant with the Virgin and Child. 16th century.
20. Pendant with Christ. 16th century.
21. Pendant with the arms of Regensburg. 15th century.
22. Pendant, pelican with young. 15th century. (Germanisches National-Museum, Nuremberg.)
23. Bronze pins, Roman period. Switzerland. (Landes-Museum, Zurich.)

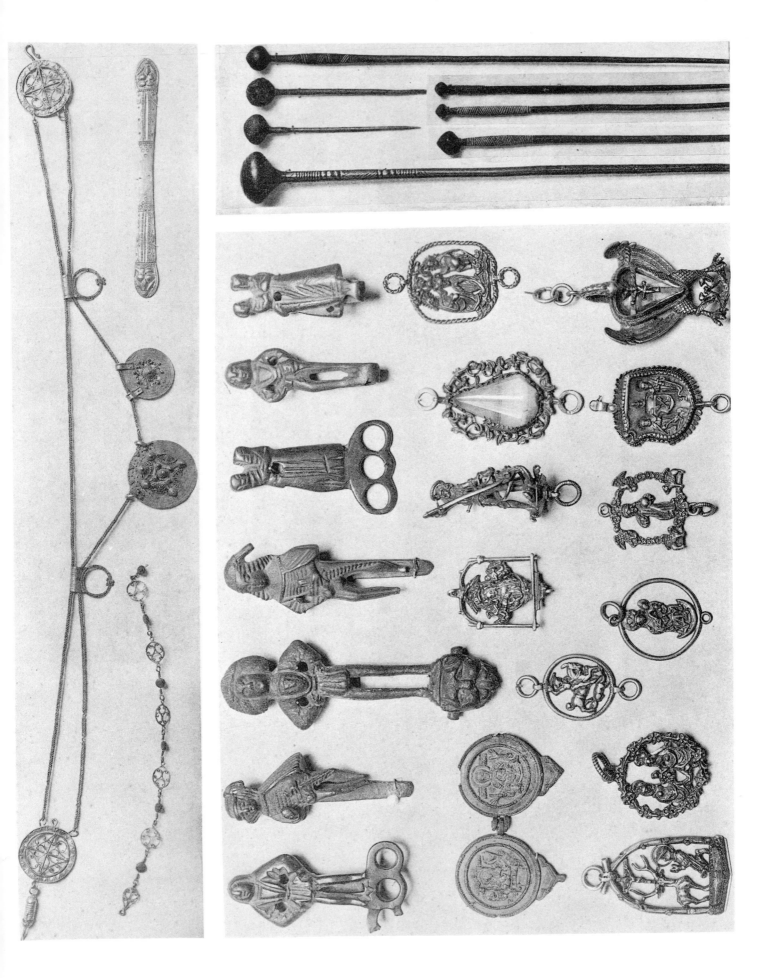

Plate 85

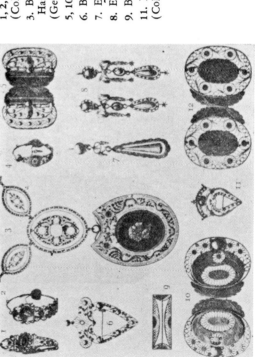

1, 2, 4. Gold earrings. East Frisia.
(Collection of Dr. Focke, Bremen.)
3. Bourgeois ornament, gold filigree chain, circa 1800. Verden,
Hanover.
(Gewerbe-Museum, Bremen.)
5, 10, 12. Breast ornaments, Syke. Harzstadt.
6. Breast ornament, Börde. Harzstadt.
7. Earring. Zelle, Hanover.
8. Earrings. Blumenthal, near Bremen.
9. Breast ornament. Harzstadt.
11. Brooch pin. Verden, Hanover.
(Collection of Dr. Focke, Bremen.)

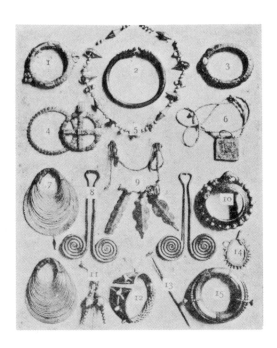

Plate 86

1, 3, 10, 15. Arm bands of the Bataks. Sumatra.

2. Arm band. Sikkim. Northern India.

4. Buckle of the Igorots. Philippines.

5. Necklace of the Bataks. Sumatra.

6. Amulet container, Atjeh. Sumatra.

7. Earring of the Dayaks. Borneo.

8. Earring of the Bataks. Sumatra.

9. Necklace of the Igorots. Philippines.

11. Ear ornaments of the Bataks. Sumatra.

12. Arm band of the Lampongs. Sumatra.

13. Ornamental pin. Sumatra.

14. Earring. Sumatra.

(Naturhistorisches Museum, Vienna, Ethnographic Collection.)

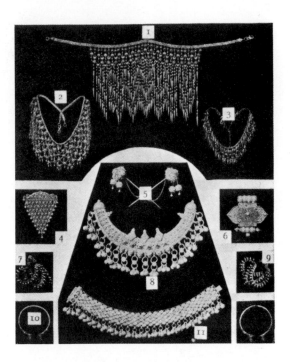

Plate 87

1, 2. Silver filigree necklaces, 1889. India (Burma).

3. Necklace, 1890, red-tinted gold. India (Burma).

4. Silver filigree brooch, 1885. Egypt.

5. Silver filigree hair pins, 1860. India.

6. Part of an ornament (pendant), 19th century, silver. India (Darjeeling).

7, 9. Arm bands, 19th century, 3 woolen cords with little brass balls. India.

8. Silvered necklace, 19th century. India.

10. Silver gilt arm clasp, 19th century. India (Bombay).

11. Ankle band, 19th century, silvered. India.
(Kunstgewerbe-Museum, Berlin.)

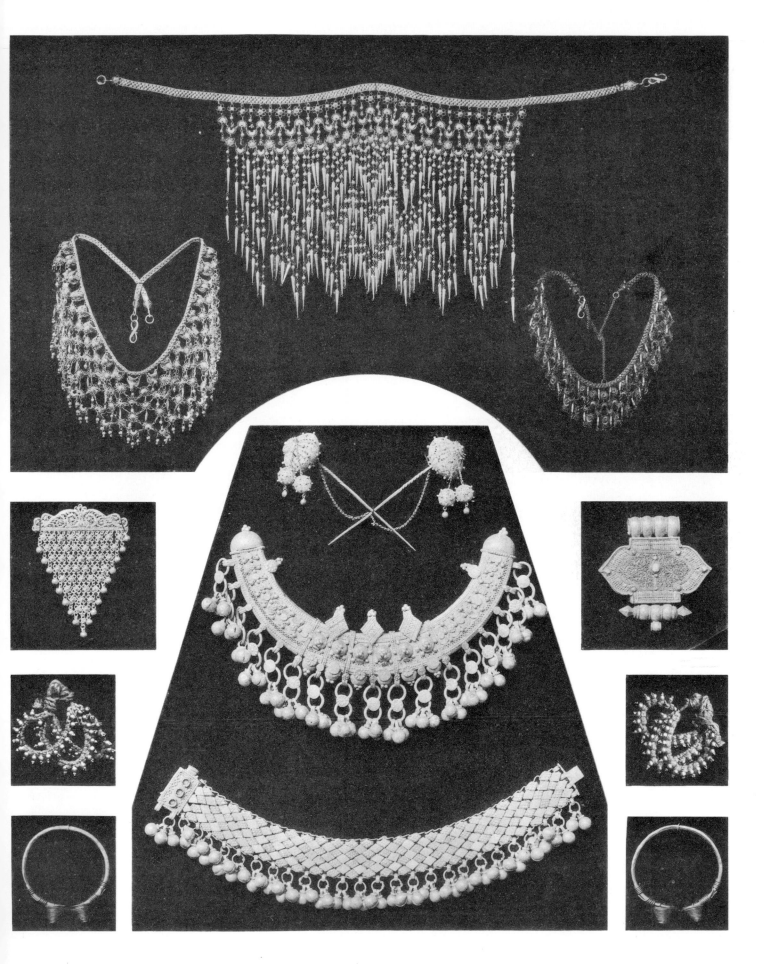

Plate 88

1–9. Silver rings with deer's teeth and colored stones. Bavaria. (Collection of A. Merklein, goldsmith, Nuremberg.)

10. Silver necklace with filigree and medals. Acquired in Nuremberg. Bavaria.

11. Anchor emblem, gilded copper. 18th century. Bavaria. (Collection of Privy Councillor M. Rosenberg, Karlsruhe.)

12, 14. Clasps of silver and filigree work. Bavaria.

13. Segmented clasp, engraved, gilded, Nuremberg workmanship. Bavaria.

15. Silver buckle, Nuremberg workmanship.

16. Silver filigree ornament, partially gilded. (Collection of A. Merklein, goldsmith, Nuremberg.)

17. Roman buckle.

18. Roman rings. (British Museum, London.)

19. Silver clasp with colored stones.

20. Silver filigree ornament, partially gilded. (Collection of A. Merklein, goldsmith, Nuremberg.)

176

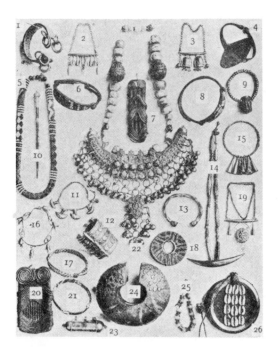

Plate 89

1. Arm band, iron. North Africa.

2, 3. Iron neck ornaments. Equatorial East Africa.

4. Iron head band. Madi, Upper White Nile region.

5. Bead necklace. Equatorial East Africa.

6, 8. Leather neckbands adorned with circlets of bone. Upper White Nile region.

7. Ornament. Africa.

9. Neck band. Equatorial East Africa.

10. Hair pin. North Africa.

11. Iron and leather neck band. Bari, Upper White Nile region.

12. Brass arm ornament. Benin.

13. Arm band. Upper White Nile region.

14–17. Neck ornaments. Equatorial East Africa.

18. Arm band, wood with brass inlay. Equatorial East Africa.

19, 21. Neck ornaments. North Africa.

20. Ornament. Africa.

22. Breast pendant. North Africa.

23. Amulet pendant. North Africa.

24. Arm band, wood with brass inlay. Equatorial East Africa.

25. Necklace, snake vertebrae and pearls. Africa.

26. Breast ornament. Madi, Upper White Nile region.

(Museum für Völkerkunde, Leipzig.)

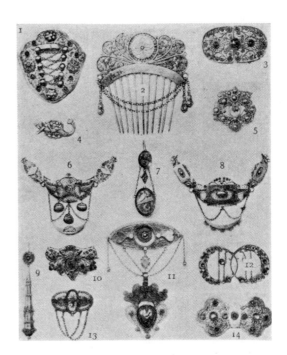

Plate 90

1. Belt buckle with filigree and chain. 18th century. Stader Geet.
2. Comb, silver with filigree. 18th century. Aurich, Frisia.
3. Belt clasp with silver filigree. 18th century. Schleswig.
4. Silver bodice hook. Schleswig.
5. Silver filigree cloak clasp. Lower Elbe.
6. Silver gilt filigree ornament. Flemish.
7. Filigree earring. Northern Germany.
8. Center piece of necklace. East Frisia.
9. Gold earring. 17th century. Jever, Oldenburg.
10. Gold brooch. Holland.
11. Two-part gold pendant, filigree work. Flemish.
12. Earrings with gold filigree. 18th century. Jever, Oldenburg.
13. Gold filigree brooch. 18th century. East Frisia.
14. Silver filigree belt clasp. Hanover.
(North Bohemian Commerce Museum, Reichenberg [Liberec], Bohemia.)

Plate 91

1, 5. Silver shirt clasps. Norway.
2. Silver shirt clasp. Norway.
3. Silver earring. Balkan Peninsula.
4, 7. Silver filigree buttons.
6. Silver fibula.
8. Ornament.
(Museum für Völkerkunde, Leipzig.)
9. Rosary with ebony beads. Southern Germany.
10, 15. Silver earrings. Dalmatia.
11. Silver gilt earrings. 17th century. Southern Germany.
12. Silver pendant. 1880. Southern Germany.
13. Gold pendant. 17th century. Southern Germany.
14. Silver gilt earring. 17th century.
16. Silver gilt necklace with jasper inlays. 17th century. Southern Germany.
(Kunstgewerbe-Museum, Dresden.)

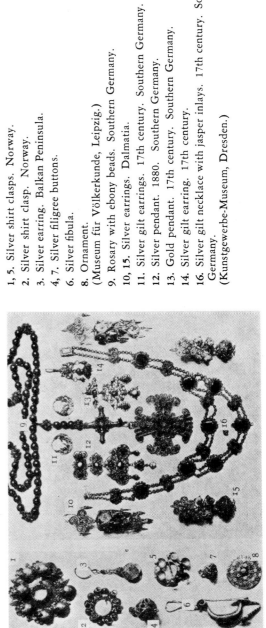

Plate 92

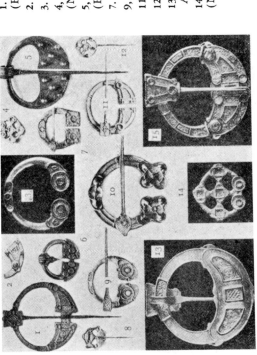

1. Gilded bronze brooch. Anglo-Saxon. (British Museum, London.)
2. Brooch, fragment, silver with gold, filigree. Anglo-Saxon.
3. Silver filigree brooch. Anglo-Saxon.
4, 8. Silver brooches. Anglo-Saxon. (National Museum, Edinburgh.)
5, 6. Silver filigree brooches. Anglo-Saxon. (British Museum, London.)
7. Bronze brooch. Anglo-Saxon.
9, 10. Silver gilt filigree brooches. Anglo-Saxon.
11. Bronze filigree brooch. Anglo-Saxon.
12. Silver brooch with amber. Anglo-Saxon.
13, 15. Obverse and reverse of a silver gilt brooch with amber. Anglo-Saxon.
14. Bronze brooch. Orkney Islands. (National Museum, Edinburgh.)

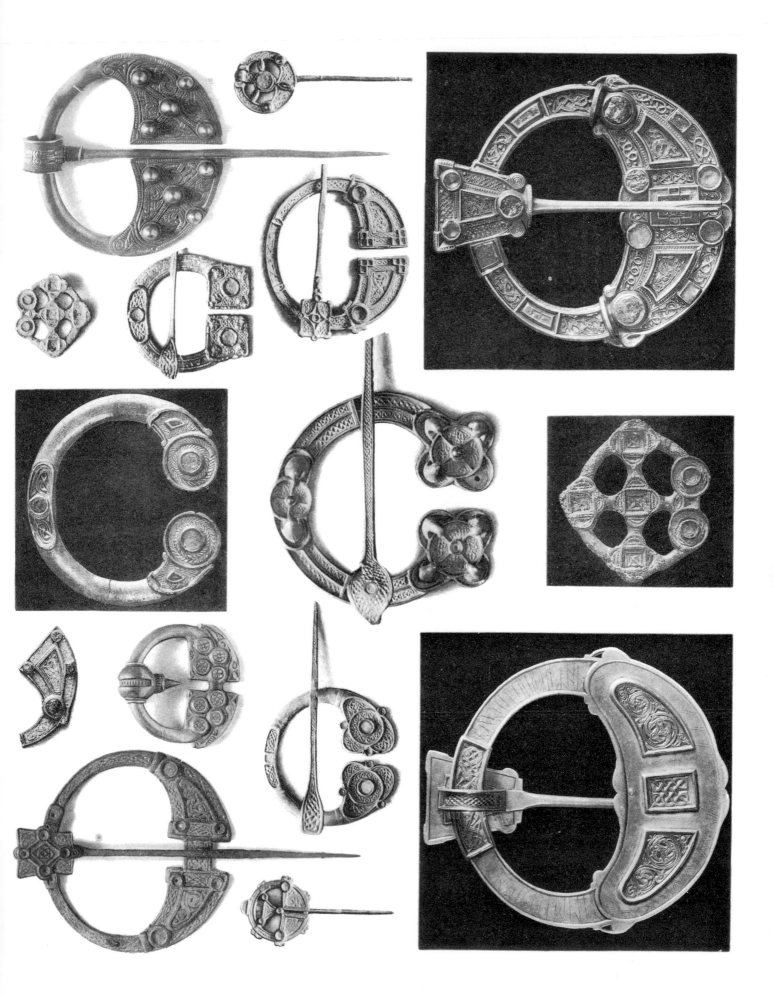

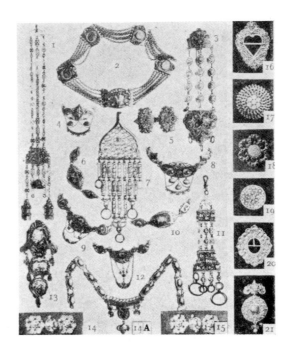

Plate 93

1. Silver ornamental chain. Southern Germany.

2. Silver necklace. Northern Germany.

3. Silver ornamental chain. Southern Germany.

4, 6, 9, 12, 13. Gold neck ornaments. Northern Germany.

5. Silver clasp. Southern Germany.

7. Iron pendant. Germany.

8. Silver gilt neck ornament. Northern Germany.

10. Silver gilt neck ornament. Northern Germany.

11. Gilded brass ornamental chain. Southern Germany. (Kunstgewerbe-Museum, Dresden.)

14, 15. Silver clasps set with coral beads (found in Pritzwalk), around 1400. Brandenburg Marches.

14A. Silver gilt necklace. Germany.

16. Silver gilt clasp, 18th to 19th century. Southern Germany.

17. Brooch with 7 medallions bearing the attributes of the 7 Ionic islands. 1873. Greece.

18. Silver gilt clasp (found in Pritzwalk), around 1400. Brandenburg Marches.

19. Snuff box. Beginning of the 18th century. Germany.

20. Silver gilt clasp. 18th to 19th century. Southern Germany.

21. Silver gilt pendant with red stones. 18th century. Southern Germany.

(Kunstgewerbe-Museum, Berlin.)

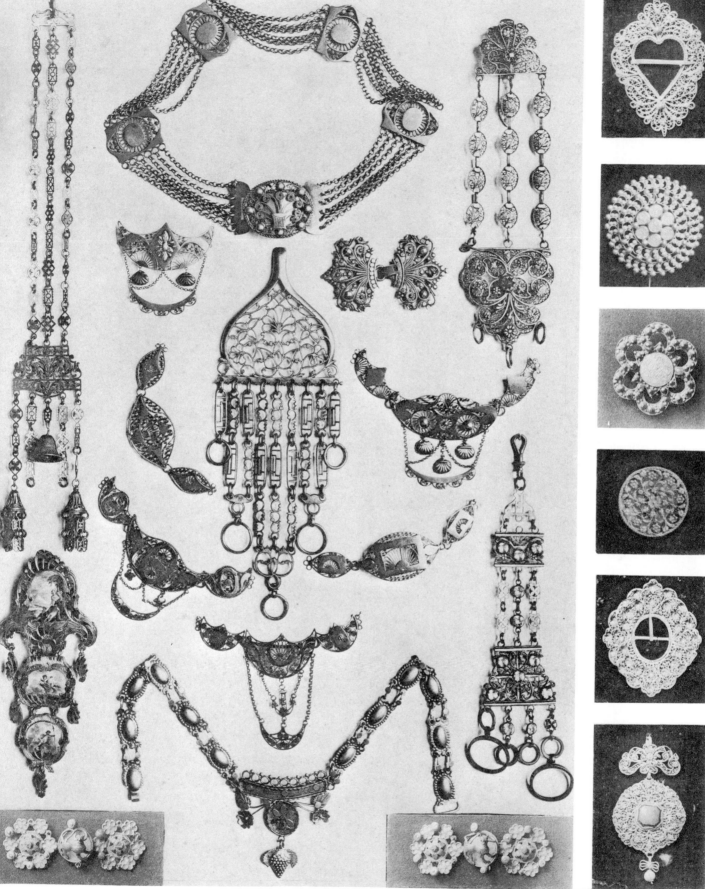

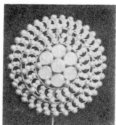

Plate 94

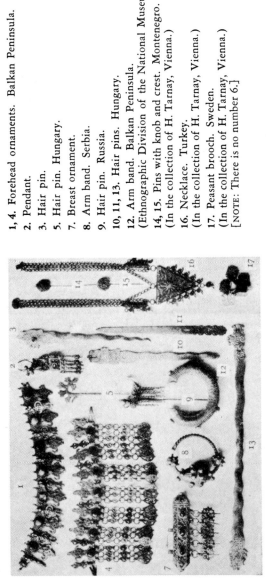

1, 4. Forehead ornaments. Balkan Peninsula.
2. Pendant.
3. Hair pin.
5. Hair pin. Hungary.
7. Breast ornament.
8. Arm band. Serbia.
9. Hair pin. Russia.
10, 11, 13. Hair pins. Hungary.
12. Arm band. Balkan Peninsula.
(Ethnographic Division of the National Museum, Budapest.)
14, 15. Pins with knob and crest. Montenegro.
(In the collection of H. Tarnay, Vienna.)
16. Necklace. Turkey.
(In the collection of H. Tarnay, Vienna.)
17. Peasant brooch. Sweden.
(In the collection of H. Tarnay, Vienna.)
[NOTE: There is no number 6.]

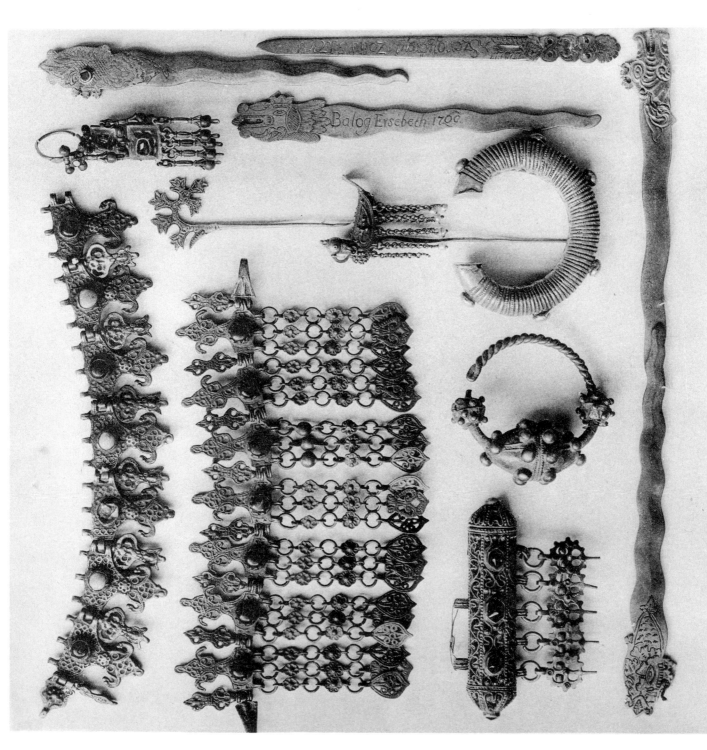

Plate 95

1. Bronze fibula, Gallo-Roman period. Wendish.
2. Bronze trimmings, Gallo-Roman period. Wendish.
3. Bronze trimmings, Gallo-Roman period. Basel.
4, 5, 23, 25. Bronze pendants, Gallo-Roman period. Wollishofen, near Zurich.
6. Bronze fibula, Gallo-Roman period. Baden (Aargau).
7. Bronze buckle, Gallo-Roman period. Giubiasco.
8–10. Bronze fibulas, Gallo-Roman period. Giubiasco and Molinazzo.
11, 15. Bronze pendants, Gallo-Roman period. Cerinasca.
11A. Bronze belt with pendant. Gallo-Roman period.
12. Bronze fibula, Gallo-Roman period. Molinazzo.
13. Bronze fibula, Gallo-Roman period. Giubiasco.
14. Bronze arm band, Gallo-Roman period. (?)
16. Belt with bronze pendant, Gallo-Roman period. Giubiasco.
17. Silver arm band, Gallo-Roman period. Giubiasco.
18. Bronze belt catch, Gallo-Roman period. Giubiasco.
19. Bronze buckle tongue (Alemannic). Unter-Embrach.
20. Bronze arm band, Gallo-Roman period. Giubiasco.
21, 22. Bronze buckles (Wendish), Gallo-Roman period. Zurich.
24. Silver arm band, Gallo-Roman period. Giubiasco.
26. Large bronze fibula, Gallo-Roman period. Giubiasco. (Landes-Museum, Zurich.)

190

Plate 96

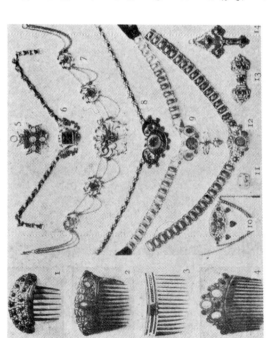

1. Comb with brass top set with carnelians. 18th century. Italy.

2. Comb with gilded brass top set with carnelians. Beginning of the 19th century. Bohemia.
(Náprstek Museum, Prague.)

3. Comb. Lusatia.
(Kunstgewerbe-Museum, Dresden.)

4. Comb with gilded brass top, with carnelians and inlaid Wedgwood porcelain medallions.
(Náprstek Museum, Prague.)

5. Cross, refined gold filigree, set with 5 chrysoprases. Beginning of the 19th century. Breslau.

6. Necklace of refined gold, center piece of elegant filigree work. Beginning of the 19th century. Grafschaft Glatz.

7. Refined gold necklace, inlaid emblem of burnished gold. Beginning of the 19th century. Breslau.
(Collection of Frau von Minkwitz, Breslau.)

8. Refined gold filigree necklace. 19th century. Grafschaft Glatz.

9. Necklace, the center piece silver filigree with inlaid burnished silver platelets. Beginning of the 19th century. Neisse (Silesia).

10. Necklace, the center piece refined gold filigree with inlaid gold platelets. Lower Silesia.

11. Silver clasp, moulded and engraved. End of the 18th century. Breslau.

12. Necklace, refined gold filigree with bossed flowers. Circa 1830. Grafschaft Glatz.

13. Clasp of raised silver, a chrysoprase in the rosette. End of the 18th century. Grafschaft Glatz.

14. Silver cross, pendant, set with four garnets. Mid-18th century. (Collection of T. Schmitz, engraver, Breslau.)

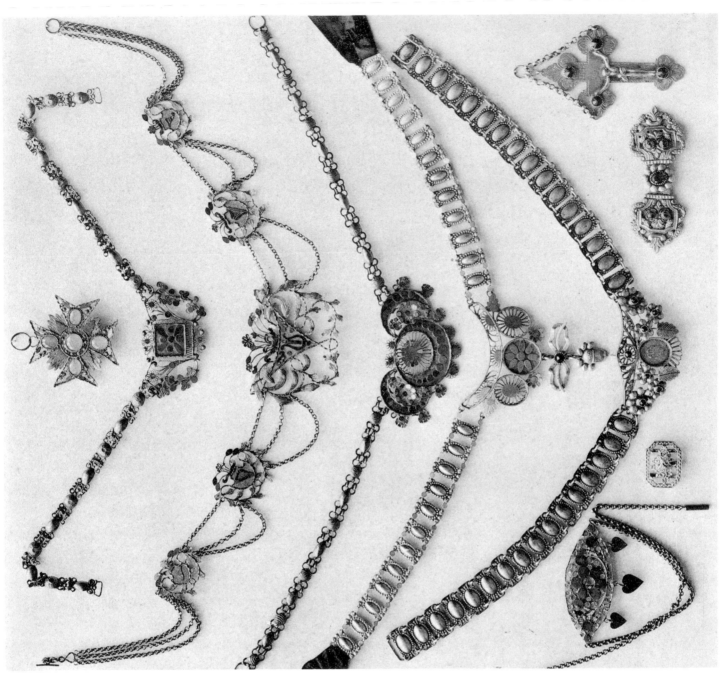

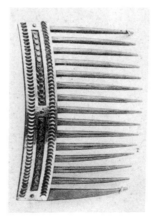

Plate 97

1. Arm band for the upper arm, silver gilt, flocks of wool and leather. Worn by Albanian watchmen in Turkish homes. Turkey.

2, 4. Earrings. Caucasus.

3. Breast ornament. Turkey.

5. Forehead ornament. Greece.

(Collection of Privy Councillor M. Rosenberg, Karlsruhe.)

Plate 98

1. Gold filigree earring. 17th to 18th century. Venice.
2, 17. Gilded silver filigree chatelaines. 18th to 19th century. Southern Germany.
3, 18. Silver filigree earrings with turquoises. 18th century. Venice.
(Kunstgewerbe-Museum, Berlin.)
4–12, 14. Silver gilt earrings. 19th century. Italy.
13. Silver gilt earring. 19th century. India.
(Österreichisches Museum für Kunst und Industrie, Vienna.)
15. Silver gilt brooch. 18th to 19th century. Southern Germany.
16. Earring, gold filigree and pearls. 17th to 18th century. Venice.
(Kunstgewerbe-Museum, Berlin.)
19–28. Silver filigree ornaments. Silesia.
(Museum für Österreichische Volkskunde, Vienna.)

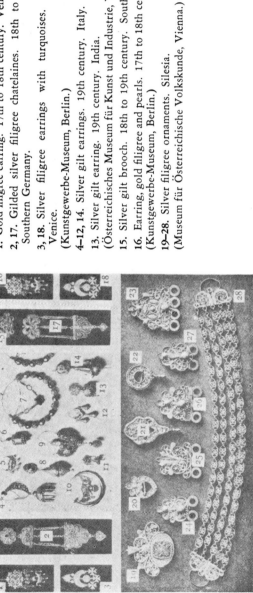

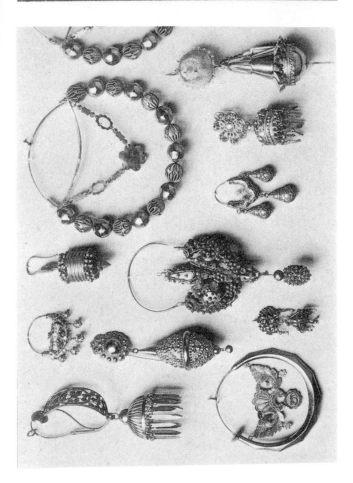

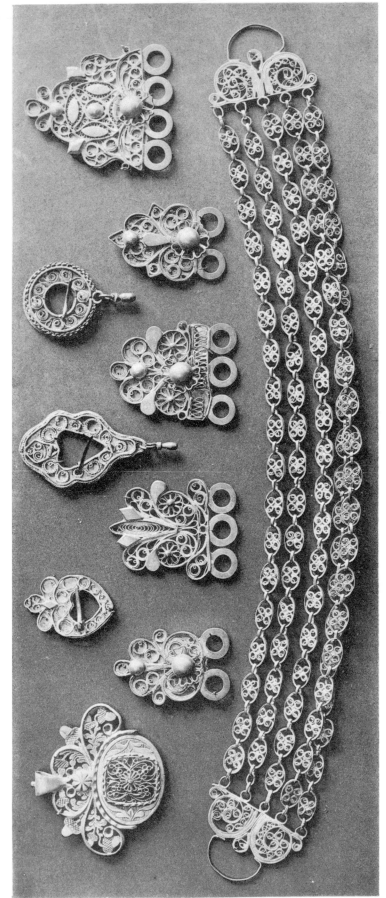

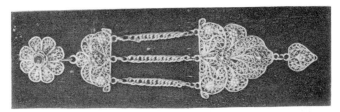

Plate 99

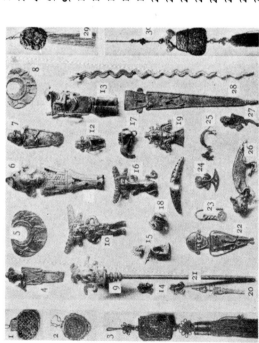

1, 3, 30. Perfume containers worn as breast ornaments. Korea.
2. Ornamental medallion. Korea.
4, 6, 7, 12, 22. Gold figures. Colombia (Bogotá).
5, 8. Nose ornaments of gold plate. Colombia (Antioquia).
9, 10. Gold ornaments, reproductions. Colombia.
13. Gold figure with animal's face. Colombia (Sogamoso).
14, 21. Gold frogs. Colombia.
15. Ornament, man's head with bird. Colombia.
16, 17, 19. Gold figures, reproductions. Colombia.
18. Gold ornament for the wings of the nose. Colombia.
20. Gold implement, quiver with arrow. Colombia.
23. Gold ear ornament. Colombia.
24. Gold frog figure. Colombia.
25. Gold animal figure. Colombia.
26. Animal figure (dragon). Colombia.
27. Gold figure (woman with child). Colombia.
28. Gold snake. Colombia.
29. Carved wood fan ornament. Korea.
(Museum für Völkerkunde, Leipzig.)
[NOTE: There is no number 11.]

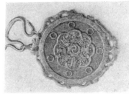

Plate 100

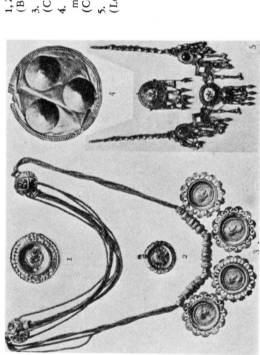

1, 2. Roman gold ornaments. Italy. (British Museum, London.)

3. Roman woman's necklace, refined gold. Egypt. (Collection of Adolf Bachofen von Echt, Nussdorf, Vienna.)

4. Ornamental disc (gold) found in Hungary (period of migrations). (Collection of Privy Councillor M. Rosenberg, Karlsruhe.)

5. Roman brooch and breast ornament, gold. Italy. (Louvre, Paris.)

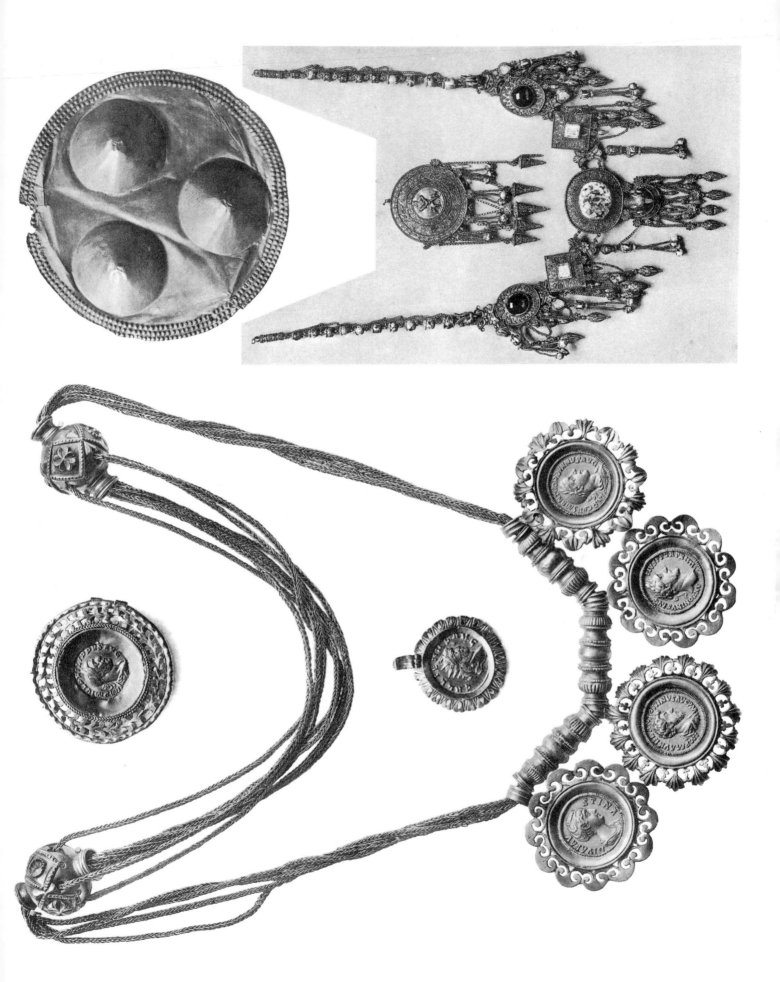

Plate 101

1. Gilded bronze pendant. 17th century. Barcelona.
2. Brass arm band with coral beads. Krumau (Bohemia).
3. Brass pendant. 17th century. Barcelona.
4. Brass earrings. 17th century. Barcelona.
5, 6, 9, 14. Bronze pendants. 17th century. Barcelona.
7. Silver filigree cross for the neck. 17th century.
8, 10, 15. Silver filigree pendants. 17th century.
11. Bronze earring. 17th century. Barcelona.
12. Silver earring. Barcelona.
13. Silver ornament with coral beads. Arabia.
(Moravian Commerce Museum, Brno.)

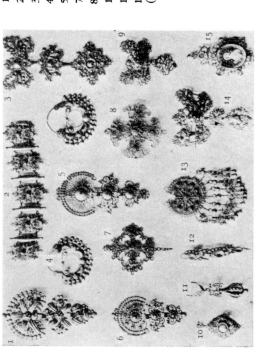

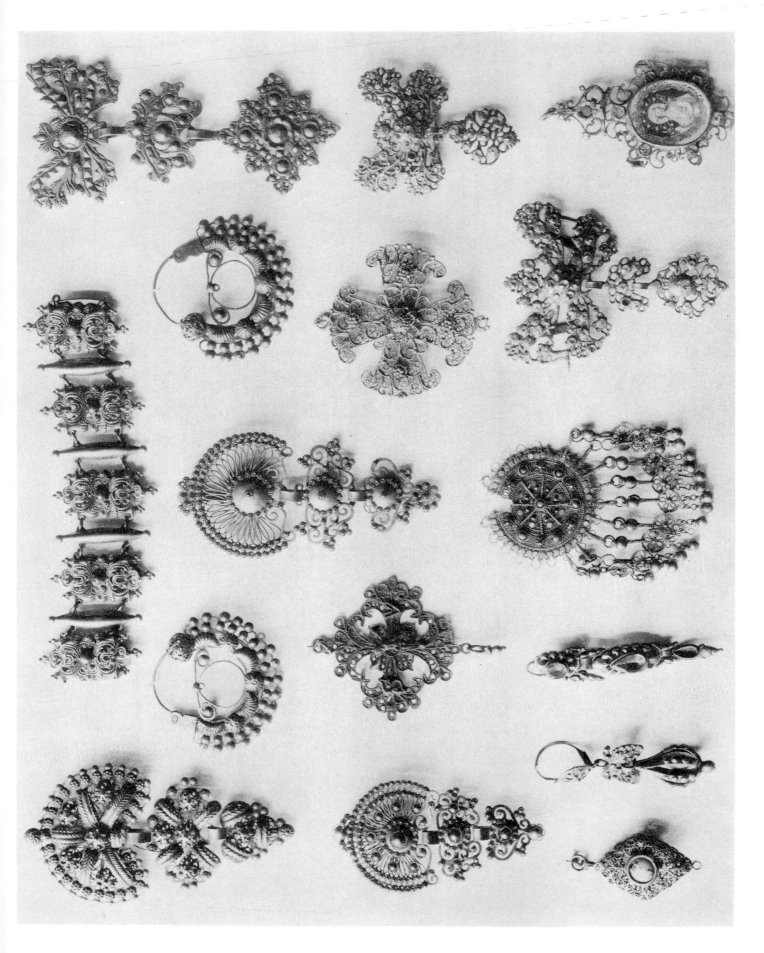

Plate 102

1. Silver gilt necklace with glass jewels. South Slavic.
2. Arm band, silver gilt. South Slavic.
3. Silver gilt pendant in the shape of a shield, with colored vitreous paste. Italian.
4. Silver gilt pendant. 16th century. Italian.
5. Silver filigree belt clasp with colored vitreous paste. Oriental.
6. Gilded brass pendant. 17th century.
7. Bedouin necklace, silver with coral beads. Sana (Southern Arabia).
8. Silver gilt earring. Southern Slavic.
9. Breast ornament, silver with coral beads. Arabian.
(Moravian Commerce Museum, Brno.)

Plate 103

1, 2. Center pieces of so-called plate chains, ducat gold, first half of the 19th century, folk jewelry. Silesia.
(Schlesisches Museum für Kunstgewerbe und Altertümer, Breslau.)

3. Silver gilt belt buckle. Hanover.
(Collection of Dr. Focke, Bremen.)

4. Breast buckle. Gilded silver filigree with turquoises. 18th century. Altenland.

5. Silver shoe buckle. 18th to 19th century. Altenland.

6. Raised silver belt clasp. 18th century.

7. Heart-shaped clasp (Hartje). Around 1765. Heligoland.
(Gewerbe-Museum, Bremen.)

8. Pendant, ducat gold. End of the 18th century. Silesia.
(Schlesisches Museum für Kunstgewerbe und Altertümer, Breslau.)

9. Silver gilt belt buckle. Wesermarsch.
(Gewerbe-Museum, Bremen.)

10. Clasp with 6 ruby-red glass drops. Jübeck, Schleswig.
(Museum für Kunst und Gewerbe, Hamburg.)

Plate 104

1. Gold filigree fibula. 400 B.C. Greek-Italic.
(Kunstgewerbeschule, Vienna.)

2. Necklace, cast brass, after Etruscan originals. Produced at the
end of the 19th century. Vienna.
(Kunstgewerbliche Fachschule, Gablonz.)

3. Earring, electrodeposit reproduction of an ancient ornament
from the Vettersfelde gold hoard. Brandenburg Marches.

4–6. Discs with relief ornament, electrodeposit reproductions, ca.
1000 B.C.
(Kunstgewerbeschule, Vienna.)

7, 9. Silver fibulas covered with gold plate. Szilágysomlyó,
Transylvania.

8. Gold fibula. Szilágysomlyó.

10. Fibula of white gold. Szilágysomlyó, Transylvania.

11. Silver fibula covered with gold plate. Szilágysomlyó,
Transylvania.
(National Museum, Budapest.)

Plate 105

1, 4, 6, 7, 9, 10, 11, 15, 17, 19, 28, 33. Hair pins. Korea.
2, 3, 5, 8, 12, 16, 20, 21, 22, 23, 29, 30, 34. Earrings. Korea.
13, 14, 24, 25, 26, 27, 32. Parts of ornaments. Korea.
18, 31. Arm bands. Korea.
35. Ring. Korea.
(Museum für Völkerkunde, Leipzig.)

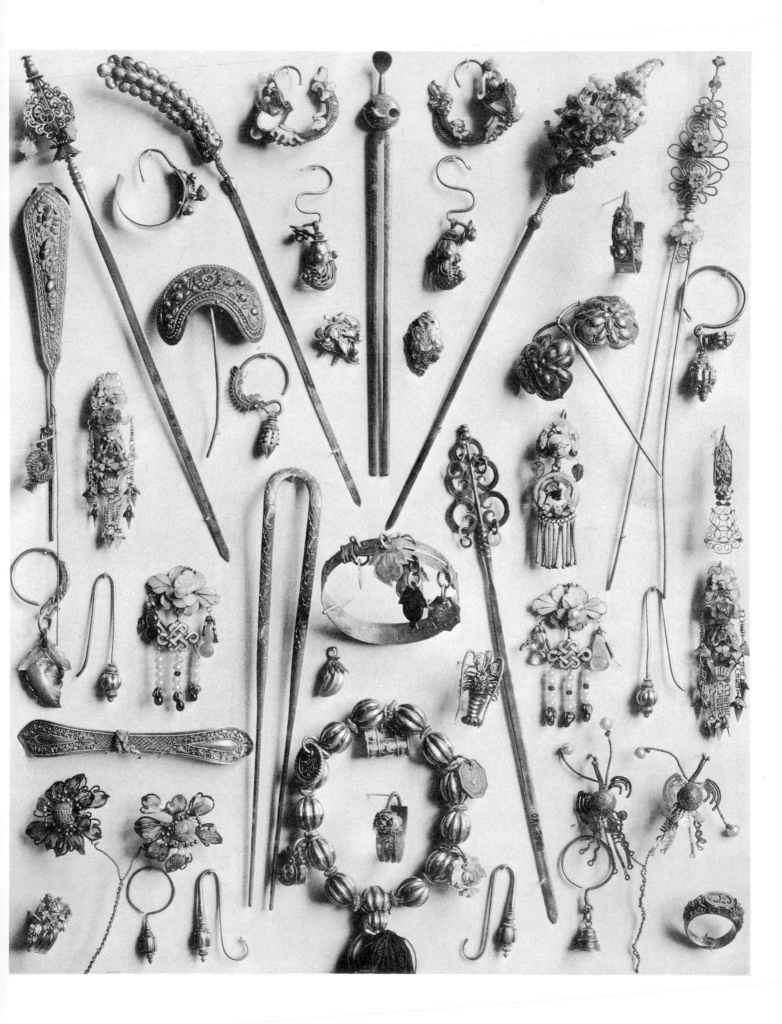

Plate 106

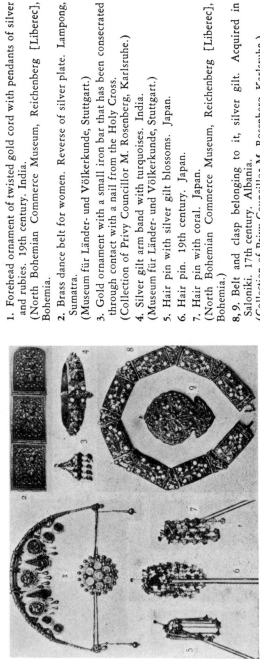

1. Forehead ornament of twisted gold cord with pendants of silver and rubies. 19th century. India.
(North Bohemian Commerce Museum, Reichenberg [Liberec], Bohemia.

2. Brass dance belt for women. Reverse of silver plate. Lampong, Sumatra.
(Museum für Länder- und Völkerkunde, Stuttgart.)

3. Gold ornament with a small iron bar that has been consecrated through contact with a nail from the Holy Cross.
(Collection of Privy Councillor M. Rosenberg, Karlsruhe.)

4. Silver gilt arm band with turquoises. India.
(Museum für Länder- und Völkerkunde, Stuttgart.)

5. Hair pin with silver gilt blossoms. Japan.

6. Hair pin. 19th century. Japan.

7. Hair pin with coral. Japan.
(North Bohemian Commerce Museum, Reichenberg [Liberec], Bohemia.)

8, 9. Belt and clasp belonging to it, silver gilt. Acquired in Saloniki. 17th century. Albania.
(Collection of Privy Councillor M. Rosenberg, Karlsruhe.)

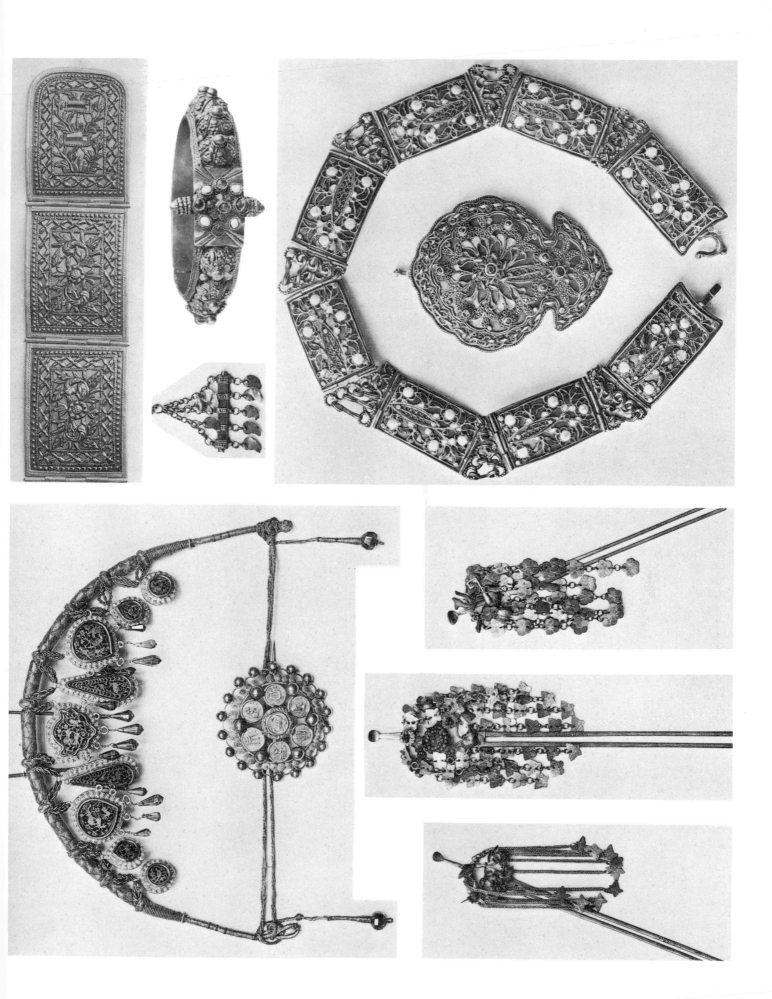

Plate 107

1. Silver filigree clasp, gilded and enamelled. Orient. (Kunstgewerbe-Museum, Berlin.)

2. Silver filigree belt clasp from the costume of a Cossack hetman. 18th century. 110 mm high. Russia. (Kunsthistorisches Museum, Vienna.)

3. Silver gilt filigree clasp. Greece.

4. Silver gilt clasp with coral. Danube provinces.

5, 7. Silver gilt filigree jewelry. Norway. (Kunstgewerbe-Museum, Berlin.)

6. Engraved brass belt clasp. Bosnia.

8. Brass belt clasp with mosaic work, engraved. Bosnia. (Náprstek Museum, Prague.)

9. Dolman buttons of raised silver and filigree. 18th century. Hungary. (Kunsthistorisches Museum, Vienna.)

10. Belt clasp, brass, enamel. Bulgaria. (Náprstek Museum, Prague.)

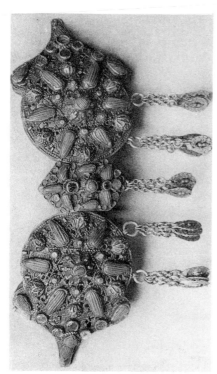

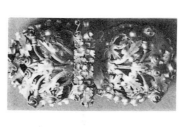

Plate 108

1. Three-sided gold necklace. Oldenburgisches Münsterland.
(Collection of Dr. Focke, Bremen.)

2. Silver necklace. Broistedt near Brunswick.
(Neues Städtisches Museum, Brunswick.)

3. Part of a clasp. Neighborhood of Lüneburg.
(Collection of Dr. Focke, Bremen.)

4. Silver buckle. 18th century. Bavaria.
(Collection of A. Merklein, goldsmith, Nuremberg.)

5. Silver gilt necklace. Volkmarode, near Brunswick.
(Neues Städtisches Museum, Brunswick.)

6, 8. Parts of triple clasps, gold. Frisia.
(Collection of Dr. Focke, Bremen.)

7. Shoe buckle, sheet silver. Ölper.
(Neues Städtisches Museum, Brunswick.)

9, 10. Parts of clasps, gold. Oldenburgisches Münsterland.
(Collection of Dr. Focke, Bremen.)

11, 13. Silver gilt buckles. Brunswick.

12. Silver necklace. Drütle, near Brunswick.
(Neues Städtisches Museum, Brunswick.)

I. Jewish wedding rings, gold with filigree. 16th to 17th century. Italy.

II. Gold rings. 16th to 18th century. Germany.

III. Eight gold rings. 16th to 18th century. Italy.
One ring, gold and silver. England.
One gold ring. Orient.
One gold ring. Etruscan.

IV. Rings, gold, silver with enamel painting. 16th to 18th century. France.

Plate 109

V. Roman gold rings.
(Grossherzoglich Badische Kunstgewerbeschule, Pforzheim.)

I.

II.

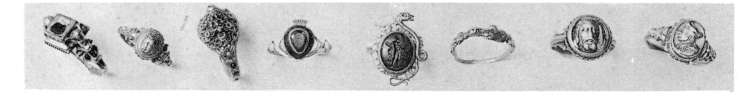

III.

IV.

V.

Dover Books on Art

AN ATLAS OF ANIMAL ANATOMY FOR ARTISTS, W. Ellenberger, H. Baum, H. Dittrich. The largest, richest animal anatomy for artists in English. Form, musculature, tendons, bone structure, expression, detailed cross sections of head, other features, of the horse, lion, dog, cat, deer, seal, kangaroo, cow, bull, goat, monkey, hare, many other animals. "Highly recommended," DESIGN. Second, revised, enlarged edition with new plates from Cuvier, Stubbs, etc. 288 illustrations. 153pp. 11⅜ x 9.

20082-5 Paperbound $3.00

ANIMAL DRAWING: ANATOMY AND ACTION FOR ARTISTS, C. R. Knight. 158 studies, with full accompanying text, of such animals as the gorilla, bear, bison, dromedary, camel, vulture, pelican, iguana, shark, etc., by one of the greatest modern masters of animal drawing. Innumerable tips on how to get life expression into your work. "An excellent reference work," SAN FRANCISCO CHRONICLE. 158 illustrations. 156pp. 10½ x 8½.

20426-X Paperbound $3.00

ARCHITECTURAL AND PERSPECTIVE DESIGNS, Giuseppe Galli Bibiena. 50 imaginative scenic drawings of Giuseppe Galli Bibiena, principal theatrical engineer and architect to the Viennese court of Charles VI. Aside from its interest to art historians, students, and art lovers, there is a whole Baroque world of material in this book for the commercial artist. Portrait of Charles VI by Martin de Meytens. 1 allegorical plate. 50 additional plates. New introduction. vi + 103pp. 10⅛ x 13¼.

21263-7 Paperbound $2.50

HANDBOOK OF DESIGNS AND DEVICES, C. P. Hornung. A remarkable working collection of 1836 basic designs and variations, all copyright-free. Variations of circle, line, cross, diamond, swastika, star, scroll, shield, many more. Notes on symbolism. "A necessity to every designer who would be original without having to labor heavily," ARTIST AND ADVERTISER. 204 plates. 240pp. 5⅜ x 8.

20125-2 Paperbound $2.00

CHINESE HOUSEHOLD FURNITURE, G. N. Kates. A summary of virtually everything that is known about authentic Chinese furniture before it was contaminated by the influence of the West. The text covers history of styles, materials used, principles of design and craftsmanship, and furniture arrangement—all fully illustrated. xiii + 190pp. 5⅝ x 8½.

20958-X Paperbound $2.00

DECORATIVE ART OF THE SOUTHWESTERN INDIANS, D. S. Sides. 300 black and white reproductions from one of the most beautiful art traditions of the primitive world, ranging from the geometric art of the Great Pueblo period of the 13th century to modern folk art. Motives from basketry, beadwork, Zuni masks, Hopi kachina dolls, Navajo sand pictures and blankets, and ceramic ware. Unusual and imaginative designs will inspire craftsmen in all media, and commercial artists may reproduce any of them without permission or payment. xviii + 101pp. 5⅝ x 8⅜.

20139-2 Paperbound $1.50

200 DECORATIVE TITLE-PAGES, edited by A. Nesbitt. Fascinating and informative from a historical point of view, this beautiful collection of decorated titles will be a great inspiration to students of design, commercial artists, advertising designers, etc. A complete survey of the genre from the first known decorated title to work in the first decades of this century. Bibliography and sources of the plates. 222pp. $8\frac{3}{8}$ x $11\frac{1}{4}$.

21264-5 Paperbound $3.50

ON THE LAWS OF JAPANESE PAINTING, H. P. Bowie. This classic work on the philosophy and technique of Japanese art is based on the author's first-hand experiences studying art in Japan. Every aspect of Japanese painting is described: the use of the brush and other materials; laws governing conception and execution; subjects for Japanese paintings, etc. The best possible substitute for a series of lessons from a great Oriental master. Index. xv + 117pp. + 66 plates. $6\frac{1}{8}$ x $9\frac{1}{4}$.

20030-2 Paperbound $2.50

A HANDBOOK OF ANATOMY FOR ART STUDENTS, Arthur Thomson. This long-popular text teaches any student, regardless of level of technical competence, all the subtleties of human anatomy. Clear photographs, numerous line sketches and diagrams of bones, joints, etc. Use it as a text for home study, as a supplement to life class work, or as a lifelong sourcebook and reference volume. Author's prefaces. 67 plates, containing 40 line drawings, 86 photographs—mostly full page. 211 figures. Appendix. Index. xx + 459pp. $5\frac{3}{8}$ x $8\frac{3}{8}$. 21163-0 Paperbound $3.50

WHITTLING AND WOODCARVING, E. J. Tangerman. With this book, a beginner who is moderately handy can whittle or carve scores of useful objects, toys for children, gifts, or simply pass hours creatively and enjoyably. "Easy as well as instructive reading," N. Y. Herald Tribune Books. 464 illustrations, with appendix and index. x + 293pp. $5\frac{1}{2}$ x $8\frac{1}{8}$.

20965-2 Paperbound $2.00

ONE HUNDRED AND ONE PATCHWORK PATTERNS, Ruby Short McKim. Whether you have made a hundred quilts or none at all, you will find this the single most useful book on quilt-making. There are 101 full patterns (all exact size) with full instructions for cutting and sewing. In addition there is some really choice folklore about the origin of the ingenious pattern names: "Monkey Wrench," "Road to California," "Drunkard's Path," "Crossed Canoes," to name a few. Over 500 illustrations. 124 pp. $7\frac{7}{8}$ x $10\frac{3}{4}$. 20773-0 Paperbound $2.00

ART AND GEOMETRY, W. M. Ivins, Jr. Challenges the idea that the foundations of modern thought were laid in ancient Greece. Pitting Greek tactile-muscular intuitions of space against modern visual intuitions, the author, for 30 years curator of prints, Metropolitan Museum of Art, analyzes the differences between ancient and Renaissance painting and sculpture and tells of the first fruitful investigations of perspective. x + 113pp. $5\frac{3}{8}$ x $8\frac{3}{8}$. 20941-5 Paperbound $1.50

GREEK REVIVAL ARCHITECTURE IN AMERICA, T. Hamlin. A comprehensive study of the American Classical Revival, its regional variations, reasons for its success and eventual decline. Profusely illustrated with photos, sketches, floor plans and sections, displaying the work of almost every important architect of the time. 2 appendices. 39 figures, 94 plates containing 221 photos, 62 architectural designs, drawings, etc. 324-item classified bibliography. Index. xi + 439pp. 5⅜ x 8½.

21148-7　Paperbound $4.50

CREATIVE LITHOGRAPHY AND HOW TO DO IT, Grant Arnold. Written by a man who practiced and taught lithography for many years, this highly useful volume explains all the steps of the lithographic process from tracing the drawings on the stone to printing the lithograph, with helpful hints for solving special problems. Index. 16 reproductions of lithographs. 11 drawings. xv + 214pp. of text. 5⅜ x 8½.

21208-4　Paperbound $3.00

TEACH YOURSELF ANTIQUE COLLECTING, E. Bradford. An excellent, brief guide to collecting British furniture, silver, pictures and prints, pewter, pottery and porcelain, Victoriana, enamels, clocks or other antiques. Much background information difficult to find elsewhere. 15pp. of illus. 215pp. 7 x 4¼.

21368-4　Clothbound $2.50

PAINTING IN THE FAR EAST, L. Binyon. A study of over 1500 years of Oriental art by one of the world's outstanding authorities. The author chooses the most important masters in each period—Wu Tao-tzu, Toba Sojo, Kanaoka, Li Lung-mien, Masanobu, Okio, etc.—and examines the works, schools, and influence of each within their cultural context. 42 photographs. Sources of original works and selected bibliography. Notes including list of principal painters by periods. xx + 297pp. 6⅛ x 9¼.

20520-7　Paperbound $5.00

THE ALPHABET AND ELEMENTS OF LETTERING, F. W. Goudy. A beautifully illustrated volume on the aesthetics of letters and type faces and their history and development. Each plate consists of 15 forms of a single letter with the last plate devoted to the ampersand and the numerals. "A sound guide for all persons engaged in printing or drawing," Saturday Review. 27 full-page plates. 48 additional figures. xii + 131pp. 7⅞ x 10¾.

20792-7　Paperbound $2.50

THE COMPLETE BOOK OF SILK SCREEN PRINTING PRODUCTION, J. I. Biegeleisen. Here is a clear and complete picture of every aspect of silk screen technique and press operation—from individually operated manual presses to modern automatic ones. Unsurpassed as a guidebook for setting up shop, making shop operation more efficient, finding out about latest methods and equipment; or as a textbook for use in teaching, studying, or learning all aspects of the profession. 124 figures. Index. Bibliography. List of Supply Sources. xi + 253pp. 5⅜ x 8½.

21100-2　Paperbound $2.75

ANIMALS IN MOTION, Eadweard Muybridge. The largest collection of animal action photos in print. 34 different animals (horses, mules, oxen, goats, camels, pigs, cats, lions, gnus, deer, monkeys, eagles—and 22 others) in 132 characteristic actions. All 3919 photographs are taken in series at speeds up to 1/1600th of a second, offering artists, biologists, cartoonists a remarkable opportunity to see exactly how an ostrich's head bobs when running, how a lion puts his foot down, how an elephant's knee bends, how a bird flaps his wings, thousands of other hard-to-catch details. "A really marvellous series of plates," NATURE. 380 full-page plates. Heavy glossy stock, reinforced binding with headbands. 7⅞ x 10¾.   20203-8   Clothbound $10.00

THE BOOK OF SIGNS, R. Koch. 493 symbols—crosses, monograms, astrological, biological symbols, runes, etc.—from ancient manuscripts, cathedrals, coins, catacombs, pottery. May be reproduced permission-free. 493 illustrations by Fritz Kredel. 104pp. 6⅛ x 9¼.   20162-7   Paperbound $1.25

A HANDBOOK OF EARLY ADVERTISING ART, C. P. Hornung. The largest collection of copyright-free early advertising art ever compiled. Vol. I: 2,000 illustrations of animals, old automobiles, buildings, allegorical figures, fire engines, Indians, ships, trains, more than 33 other categories! Vol. II: Over 4,000 typographical specimens; 600 Roman, Gothic, Barnum, Old English faces; 630 ornamental type faces; hundreds of scrolls, initials, flourishes, etc. "A remarkable collection," PRINTERS' INK.

Vol. I: Pictorial Volume. Over 2000 illustrations. 256pp. 9 x 12.   20122-8   Clothbound $10.00

Vol. II: Typographical Volume. Over 4000 specimens. 319pp. 9 x 12.   20123-6   Clothbound $10.00

Two volume set, Clothbound, only $20.00

THE UNIVERSAL PENMAN, George Bickham. Exact reproduction of beautiful 18th-century book of handwriting. 22 complete alphabets in finest English roundhand, other scripts, over 2000 elaborate flourishes, 122 calligraphic illustrations, etc. Material is copyright-free. "An essential part of any art library, and a book of permanent value," AMERICAN ARTIST. 212 plates. 224pp. 9 x 13¾.   20020-5   Clothbound $12.50

AN ATLAS OF ANATOMY FOR ARTISTS, F. Schider. This standard work contains 189 full-page plates, more than 647 illustrations of all aspects of the human skeleton, musculature, cutaway portions of the body, each part of the anatomy, hand forms, eyelids, breasts, location of muscles under the flesh, etc. 59 plates illustrate how Michelangelo, da Vinci, Goya, 15 others, drew human anatomy. New 3rd edition enlarged by 52 new illustrations by Cloquet, Barcsay. "The standard reference tool," AMERICAN LIBRARY ASSOCIATION. "Excellent," AMERICAN ARTIST. 189 plates, 647 illustrations. xxvi + 192pp. 7⅞ x 10⅝.   20241-0   Clothbound $6.50

MASTERPIECES OF FURNITURE, Verna Cook Salomonsky. Photographs and measured drawings of some of the finest examples of Colonial American, 17th century English, Windsor, Sheraton, Hepplewhite, Chippendale, Louis XIV, Queen Anne, and various other furniture styles. The textual matter includes information on traditions, characteristics, background, etc. of various pieces. 101 plates. Bibliography. 224pp. 7⅞ x 10¾.

21381-1 Paperbound $3.00

PRIMITIVE ART, Franz Boas. In this exhaustive volume, a great American anthropologist analyzes all the fundamental traits of primitive art, covering the formal element in art, representative art, symbolism, style, literature, music, and the dance. Illustrations of Indian embroidery, paleolithic paintings, woven blankets, wing and tail designs, totem poles, cutlery, earthenware, baskets and many other primitive objects and motifs. Over 900 illustrations. 376pp. 5⅜ x 8.   20025-6 Paperbound $3.00

AN INTRODUCTION TO A HISTORY OF WOODCUT, A. M. Hind. Nearly all of this authoritative 2-volume set is devoted to the 15th century—the period during which the woodcut came of age as an important art form. It is the most complete compendium of information on this period, the artists who contributed to it, and their technical and artistic accomplishments. Profusely illustrated with cuts by 15th century masters, and later works for comparative purposes. 484 illustrations. 5 indexes. Total of xi + 838pp. 5⅜ x 8½. Two-vols. 20952-0, 20953-9 Paperbound $7.00

ART STUDENTS' ANATOMY, E. J. Farris. Teaching anatomy by using chiefly living objects for illustration, this study has enjoyed long popularity and success in art courses and home-study programs. All the basic elements of the human anatomy are illustrated in minute detail, diagrammed and pictured as they pass through common movements and actions. 158 drawings, photographs, and roentgenograms. Glossary of anatomical terms. x + 159pp. 5⅝ x 8⅜.   20744-7 Paperbound $1.50

COLONIAL LIGHTING, A. H. Hayward. The only book to cover the fascinating story of lamps and other lighting devices in America. Beginning with rush light holders used by the early settlers, it ranges through the elaborate chandeliers of the Federal period, illustrating 647 lamps. Of great value to antique collectors, designers, and historians of arts and crafts. Revised and enlarged by James R. Marsh. xxxi + 198pp. 5⅝ x 8¼.

20975-X Paperbound $2.50

PINE FURNITURE OF EARLY NEW ENGLAND, R. H. Kettell. Over 400 illustrations, over 50 working drawings of early New England chairs, benches, beds, cupboards, mirrors, shelves, tables, other furniture esteemed for simple beauty and character. "Rich store of illustrations . . . emphasizes the individuality and varied design," ANTIQUES. 413 illustrations, 55 working drawings. 475pp. 8 x 10¾.   20145-7   Clothbound $10.00

BASIC BOOKBINDING, A. W. Lewis. Enables both beginners and experts to rebind old books or bind paperbacks in hard covers. Treats materials, tools; gives step-by-step instruction in how to collate a book, sew it, back it, make boards, etc. 261 illus. Appendices. 155pp. 5⅜ x 8.   20169-4   Paperbound $1.75

DESIGN MOTIFS OF ANCIENT MEXICO, J. Enciso. Nearly 90% of these 766 superb designs from Aztec, Olmec, Totonac, Maya, and Toltec origins are unobtainable elsewhere. Contains plumed serpents, wind gods, animals, demons, dancers, monsters, etc. Excellent applied design source. Originally $17.50. 766 illustrations, thousands of motifs. 192pp. 6⅛ x 9¼.
20084-1   Paperbound $2.50

A DIDEROT PICTORIAL ENCYCLOPEDIA OF TRADES AND INDUSTRY. Manufacturing and the Technical Arts in Plates Selected from "L'Encyclopédie ou Dictionnaire Raisonné des Sciences, des Arts, et des Métiers," of Denis Diderot, edited with text by C. Gillispie. Over 2000 illustrations on 485 full-page plates. Magnificent 18th-century engravings of men, women, and children working at such trades as milling flour, cheesemaking, charcoal burning, mining, silverplating, shoeing horses, making fine glass, printing, hundreds more, showing details of machinery, different steps in sequence, etc. A remarkable art work, but also the largest collection of working figures in print, copyright-free, for art directors, designers, etc. Two vols. 920pp. 9 x 12. Heavy library cloth.   22284-5, 22283-3   Two volume set $27.50

SILK SCREEN TECHNIQUES, J. Biegeleisen, M. Cohn. A practical step-by-step home course in one of the most versatile, least expensive graphic arts processes. How to build an inexpensive silk screen, prepare stencils, print, achieve special textures, use color, etc. Every step explained, diagrammed. 149 illustrations, 201pp. 6⅛ x 9¼.   20433-2   Paperbound $2.00

STICKS AND STONES, Lewis Mumford. An examination of forces influencing American architecture: the medieval tradition in early New England, the classical influence in Jefferson's time, the Brown Decades, the imperial facade, the machine age, etc. "A truly remarkable book," SAT. REV. OF LITERATURE. 2nd revised edition. 21 illus. xvii + 240pp. 5⅜ x 8.
20202-X   Paperbound $2.00

THE AUTOBIOGRAPHY OF AN IDEA, Louis Sullivan. The architect whom Frank Lloyd Wright called "the master," records the development of the theories that revolutionized America's skyline. 34 full-page plates of Sullivan's finest work. New introduction by R. M. Line. xiv + 335pp. 5⅜ x 8.
20281-X   Paperbound $2.50

ANIMALS IN MOTION, Eadweard Muybridge. The largest collection of animal action photos in print. 34 different animals (horses, mules, oxen, goats, camels, pigs, cats, lions, gnus, deer, monkeys, eagles—and 22 others) in 132 characteristic actions. All 3919 photographs are taken in series at speeds up to 1/1600th of a second, offering artists, biologists, cartoonists a remarkable opportunity to see exactly how an ostrich's head bobs when running, how a lion puts his foot down, how an elephant's knee bends, how a bird flaps his wings, thousands of other hard-to-catch details. "A really marvellous series of plates," NATURE. 380 full-page plates. Heavy glossy stock, reinforced binding with headbands. 7⅞ x 10¾.　　　　　20203-8　Clothbound $12.50

THE BOOK OF SIGNS, R. Koch. 493 symbols—crosses, monograms, astrological, biological symbols, runes, etc.—from ancient manuscripts, cathedrals, coins, catacombs, pottery. May be reproduced permission-free. 493 illustrations by Fritz Kredel. 104pp. 6⅛ x 9¼.　　　　　20162-7　Paperbound $1.50

A HANDBOOK OF EARLY ADVERTISING ART, C. P. Hornung. The largest collection of copyright-free early advertising art ever compiled. Vol. I: 2,000 illustrations of animals, old automobiles, buildings, allegorical figures, fire engines, Indians, ships, trains, more than 33 other categories! Vol. II: Over 4,000 typographical specimens; 600 Roman, Gothic, Barnum, Old English faces; 630 ornamental type faces; hundreds of scrolls, initials, flourishes, etc. "A remarkable collection," PRINTERS' INK.
Vol. I: Pictorial Volume. Over 2000 illustrations. 256pp. 9 x 12.
　　　　　20122-8　Clothbound $12.50
Vol. II: Typographical Volume. Over 4000 specimens. 319pp.
9 x 12.　　　　　20123-6　Clothbound $12.50
　　　Two volume set, Clothbound, only $25.00

THE UNIVERSAL PENMAN, George Bickham. Exact reproduction of beautiful 18th-century book of handwriting. 22 complete alphabets in finest English roundhand, other scripts, over 2000 elaborate flourishes, 122 calligraphic illustrations, etc. Material is copyright-free. "An essential part of any art library, and a book of permanent value," AMERICAN ARTIST. 212 plates. 224pp. 9 x 13¾.　　　　20616-5 Paperbound $5.00

AN ATLAS OF ANATOMY FOR ARTISTS, F. Schider. This standard work contains 189 full-page plates, more than 647 illustrations of all aspects of the human skeleton, musculature, cutaway portions of the body, each part of the anatomy, hand forms, eyelids, breasts, location of muscles under the flesh, etc. 59 plates illustrate how Michelangelo, da Vinci, Goya, 15 others, drew human anatomy. New 3rd edition enlarged by 52 new illustrations by Cloquet, Barcsay. "The standard reference tool," AMERICAN LIBRARY ASSOCIATION. "Excellent," AMERICAN ARTIST. 189 plates, 647 illustrations. xxvi + 192pp. 7⅞ x 10⅝.　　　　　20241-0　Clothbound $6.95

VASARI ON TECHNIQUE, G. Vasari. Pupil of Michelangelo, outstanding biographer of Renaissance artists reveals technical methods of his day. Marble, bronze, fresco painting, mosaics, engraving, stained glass, rustic ware, etc. Only English translation, extensively annotated by G. Baldwin Brown. 18 plates. 342pp. 5⅜ x 8.   20717-X Paperbound $3.50

FOOT-HIGH LETTERS: A GUIDE TO LETTERING, M. Price. 28 15½ x 22½″ plates, give classic Roman alphabet, one foot high per letter, plus 9 other 2″ high letter forms for each letter. 16 page syllabus. Ideal for lettering classes, home study. 28 plates in box.   20238-9 $7.50

A HANDBOOK OF WEAVES, G. H. Oelsner. Most complete book of weaves, fully explained, differentiated, illustrated. Plain weaves, irregular, double-stitched, filling satins; derivative, basket, rib weaves; steep, broken, herringbone, twills, lace, tricot, many others. Translated, revised by S. S. Dale; supplement on analysis of weaves. Bible for all handweavers. 1875 illustrations. 410pp. 6⅛ x 9¼.   20209-7 Clothbound $7.50

JAPANESE HOMES AND THEIR SURROUNDINGS, E. S. Morse. Classic describes, analyses, illustrates all aspects of traditional Japanese home, from plan and structure to appointments, furniture, etc. Published in 1886, before Japanese architecture was contaminated by Western, this is strikingly modern in beautiful, functional approach to living. Indispensable to every architect, interior decorator, designer. 307 illustrations. Glossary. 410pp. 5⅝ x 8⅜.   20746-3 Paperbound $3.50

THE DRAWINGS OF HEINRICH KLEY. Uncut publication of long-sought-after sketchbooks of satiric, ironic iconoclast. Remarkable fantasy, weird symbolism, brilliant technique make Kley a shocking experience to layman, endless source of ideas, techniques for artist. 200 drawings, original size, captions translated. Introduction. 136pp. 6 x 9.   20024-8 Paperbound $2.00

COSTUMES OF THE ANCIENTS, Thomas Hope. Beautiful, clear, sharp line drawings of Greek and Roman figures in full costume, by noted artist and antiquary of early 19th century. Dress, armor, divinities, masks, etc. Invaluable sourcebook for costumers, designers, first-rate picture file for illustrators, commercial artists. Introductory text by Hope. 300 plates. 6 x 9.
                        20021-3 Paperbound $2.50

EPOCHS OF CHINESE AND JAPANESE ART, E. Fenollosa. Classic study of pre-20th century Oriental art, revealing, as does no other book, the important interrelationships between the art of China and Japan and their history and sociology. Illustrations include ancient bronzes, Buddhist paintings by Kobo Daishi, scroll paintings by Toba Sojo, prints by Nobusane, screens by Korin, woodcuts by Hokusai, Koryusai, Utamaro, Hiroshige and scores of other pieces by Chinese and Japanese masters. Biographical preface. Notes. Index. 242 illustrations. Total of lii + 439pp. plus 174 plates. 5⅝ x 8¼.
                        20364-6, 20265-4 Two-volume set, Paperbound $5.90

Dover Books on Art

PENNSYLVANIA DUTCH AMERICAN FOLK ART, H. J. Kauffman. The originality and charm of this early folk art give it a special appeal even today, and surviving pieces are sought by collectors all over the country. Here is a rewarding introductory guide to the Dutch country and its household art, concentrating on pictorial matter—hex signs, tulip ware, weather vanes, interiors, paintings and folk sculpture, rocking horses and children's toys, utensils, Stiegel-type glassware, etc. "A serious, worthy and helpful volume," W. G. Dooley, N. Y. TIMES. Introduction. Bibliography. 279 halftone illustrations. 28 motifs and other line drawings. 1 map. 146pp. 7⅞ x 10¾.

21205-X Paperbound $3.00

DESIGN AND EXPRESSION IN THE VISUAL ARTS, J. F. A. Taylor. Here is a much needed discussion of art theory which relates the new and sometimes bewildering directions of 20th century art to the great traditions of the past. The first discussion of principle that addresses itself to the eye rather than to the intellect, using illustrations from Rembrandt, Leonardo, Mondrian, El Greco, etc. List of plates. Index. 59 reproductions. 5 color plates. 75 figures. x + 245pp. 5⅜ x 8½.

21195-9 Paperbound $2.50

THE ENJOYMENT AND USE OF COLOR, W. Sargent. Requiring no special technical know-how, this book tells you all about color and how it is created, perceived, and imitated in art. Covers many little-known facts about color values, intensities, effects of high and low illumination, complementary colors, and color harmonies. Simple do-it-yourself experiments and observations. 35 illustrations, including 6 full-page color plates. New color frontispiece. Index. x + 274 pp. 5⅜ x 8.

20944-X Paperbound $2.75

STYLES IN PAINTING, Paul Zucker. By comparing paintings of similar subject matter, the author shows the characteristics of various painting styles. You are shown at a glance the differences between reclining nudes by Giorgione, Velasquez, Goya, Modigliani; how a Byzantine portrait is unlike a portrait by Van Eyck, da Vinci, Dürer, or Marc Chagall; how the painting of landscapes has changed gradually from ancient Pompeii to Lyonel Feininger in our own century. 241 beautiful, sharp photographs illustrate the text. xiv + 338 pp. 5⅝ x 8¼.

20760-9 Paperbound $2.25

Dover publishes books on commercial art, art history, crafts, design, art classics; also books on music, literature, science, mathematics, puzzles and entertainments, chess, engineering, biology, philosophy, psychology, languages, history, and other fields. For free circulars write to Dept. DA, Dover Publications, Inc., 180 Varick St., New York, N.Y. 10014.

ART ANATOMY, Dr. William Rimmer. One of the few books on art anatomy that are themselves works of art, this is a faithful reproduction (rearranged for handy use) of the extremely rare masterpiece of the famous 19th century anatomist, sculptor, and art teacher. Beautiful, clear line drawings show every part of the body—bony structure, muscles, features, etc. Unusual are the sections on falling bodies, foreshortenings, muscles in tension, grotesque personalities, and Rimmer's remarkable interpretation of emotions and personalities as expressed by facial features. It will supplement every other book on art anatomy you are likely to have. Reproduced clearer than the lithographic original (which sells for $500 on up on the rare book market.) Over 1,200 illustrations. xiii + 153pp. 7¾ x 10¾.

20908-3 Paperbound $2.50

THE CRAFTSMAN'S HANDBOOK, Cennino Cennini. The finest English translation of IL LIBRO DELL' ARTE, the 15th century introduction to art technique that is both a mirror of Quatrocento life and a source of many useful but nearly forgotten facets of the painter's art. 4 illustrations. xxvii + 142pp. D. V. Thompson, translator. 5⅜ x 8.   20054-X Paperbound $2.00

THE BROWN DECADES, Lewis Mumford. A picture of the "buried renaissance" of the post-Civil War period, and the founding of modern architecture (Sullivan, Richardson, Root, Roebling), landscape development (Marsh, Olmstead, Eliot), and the graphic arts (Homer, Eakins, Ryder). 2nd revised, enlarged edition. Bibliography. 12 illustrations. xiv + 266 pp. 5⅜ x 8.

20200-3 Paperbound $2.00

THE STYLES OF ORNAMENT, A. Speltz. The largest collection of line ornament in print, with 3750 numbered illustrations arranged chronologically from Egypt, Assyria, Greeks, Romans, Etruscans, through Medieval, Renaissance, 18th century, and Victorian. No permissions, no fees needed to use or reproduce illustrations. 400 plates with 3750 illustrations. Bibliography. Index. 640pp. 6 x 9.   20577-6 Paperbound $3.75

THE ART OF ETCHING, E. S. Lumsden. Every step of the etching process from essential materials to completed proof is carefully and clearly explained, with 24 annotated plates exemplifying every technique and approach discussed. The book also features a rich survey of the art, with 105 annotated plates by masters. Invaluable for beginner to advanced etcher. 374pp. 5⅜ x 8.   20049-3 Paperbound $3.00

OF THE JUST SHAPING OF LETTERS, Albrecht Dürer. This remarkable volume reveals Albrecht Dürer's rules for the geometric construction of Roman capitals and the formation of Gothic lower case and capital letters, complete with construction diagrams and directions. Of considerable practical interest to the contemporary illustrator, artist, and designer. Translated from the Latin text of the edition of 1535 by R. T. Nichol. Numerous letterform designs, construction diagrams, illustrations. iv + 43pp. 7⅞ x 10¾.   21306-4 Paperbound $2.00

LANDSCAPE GARDENING IN JAPAN, Josiah Conder. A detailed picture of Japanese gardening techniques and ideas, the artistic principles incorporated in the Japanese garden, and the religious and ethical concepts at the heart of those principles. Preface. 92 illustrations, plus all 40 full-page plates from the Supplement. Index. xv + 299pp. 8⅜ x 11¼.

21216-5 Paperbound $4.50

DESIGN AND FIGURE CARVING, E. J. Tangerman. "Anyone who can peel a potato can carve," states the author, and in this unusual book he shows you how, covering every stage in detail from very simple exercises working up to museum-quality pieces. Terrific aid for hobbyists, arts and crafts counselors, teachers, those who wish to make reproductions for the commercial market. Appendix: How to Enlarge a Design. Brief bibliography. Index. 1298 figures. x + 289pp. 5⅜ x 8½.

21209-2 Paperbound $3.00

THE STANDARD BOOK OF QUILT MAKING AND COLLECTING, M. Ickis. Even if you are a beginner, you will soon find yourself quilting like an expert, by following these clearly drawn patterns, photographs, and step-by-step instructions. Learn how to plan the quilt, to select the pattern to harmonize with the design and color of the room, to choose materials. Over 40 full-size patterns. Index. 483 illustrations. One color plate. xi + 276pp. 6¾ x 9½.   20582-7 Paperbound $3.50

LOST EXAMPLES OF COLONIAL ARCHITECTURE, J. M. Howells. This book offers a unique guided tour through America's architectural past, all of which is either no longer in existence or so changed that its original beauty has been destroyed. More than 275 clear photos of old churches, dwelling houses, public buildings, business structures, etc. 245 plates, containing 281 photos and 9 drawings, floorplans, etc. New Index. xvii + 248pp. 7⅞ x 10¾.   21143-6 Paperbound $3.50

A HISTORY OF COSTUME, Carl Köhler. The most reliable and authentic account of the development of dress from ancient times through the 19th century. Based on actual pieces of clothing that have survived, using paintings, statues and other reproductions only where originals no longer exist. Hundreds of illustrations, including detailed patterns for many articles. Highly useful for theatre and movie directors, fashion designers, illustrators, teachers. Edited and augmented by Emma von Sichart. Translated by Alexander K. Dallas. 594 illustrations. 464pp. 5⅛ x 7⅛.

21030-8 Paperbound $3.50

Dover publishes books on commercial art, art history, crafts, design, art classics; also books on music, literature, science, mathematics, puzzles and entertainments, chess, engineering, biology, philosophy, psychology, languages, history, and other fields. For free circulars write to Dept. DA, Dover Publications, Inc., 180 Varick St., New York, N.Y. 10014.